CompTIA® A+®
Certification

A Comprehensive Approach for all 2006 Exam Objectives

CompTIA® A+® Certification: A Comprehensive Approach for all 2006 Exam Objectives

Part Number: ACS085820LG
Course Edition: 1.0

NOTICES

The logo of the CompTIA Authorized Quality Curriculum (CAQC) Program and the status of this or other training material as "Authorized" under the CompTIA Authorized Quality Curriculum Program signifies that, in CompTIA's opinion, such training material covers the content of CompTIA's related certification exam. CompTIA has not reviewed or approved the accuracy of the contents of this training material and specifically disclaims any warranties of merchantability or fitness for a particular purpose. CompTIA makes no guarantee concerning the success of persons using any such "Authorized" or other training material in order to prepare for any CompTIA certification exam.

The contents of this training material were created for the CompTIA A+ certification exam numbers 220-601, 220-602, 220-603, and 220-604, covering CompTIA certification exam objectives that were current as of 2006.

How to Become CompTIA Certified: This training material can help you prepare for and pass a related CompTIA certification exam or exams. In order to achieve CompTIA certification, you must register for and pass a CompTIA certification exam or exams. In order to become CompTIA certified, you must:

1. Select a certification exam provider. For more information, please visit **www.comptia.org/certification/general_information/test_locations.aspx**.

2. Register for and schedule a time to take the CompTIA certification exam(s) at a convenient location.

3. Read and sign the Candidate Agreement, which will be presented at the time of the exam(s). The text of the Candidate Agreement can be found at **www.comptia.org/certification/general_information/ candidate_agreement.aspx**.

4. Take and pass the CompTIA certification exam(s).

For more information about CompTIA's certifications, such as its industry acceptance, benefits, or program news, please visit **www.comptia.org/certification**.

HELP US IMPROVE OUR COURSEWARE

Your comments are important to us. Please contact us at Element K Press LLC, 1-800-478-7788, 500 Canal View Boulevard, Rochester, NY 14623, Attention: Product Planning, or through our Web site at **http://support.elementkcourseware.com**.

CompTIA is a not-for-profit Information Technology (IT) trade association. CompTIA's certifications are designed by subject matter experts across the IT industry. Each CompTIA certification is vendor-neutral, covers multiple technologies, and requires demonstrations of skills and knowledge widely sought after by the IT industry. To contact CompTIA with any questions or comments, please call 1-630–678–8300 or email **questions@comptia.org**.

CompTIA® A+® Certification: A Comprehensive Approach for all 2006 Exam Objectives

Chapter 3: PC Technician Professional Best Practices

Chapter 4: Installing and Configuring Peripheral Components

Chapter 5: Installing and Configuring System Components

Chapter 6: Maintaining and Troubleshooting Peripheral Components

Chapter 7: Troubleshooting System Components

Chapter 8: Installing and Configuring Operating Systems

Chapter 9: Maintaining and Troubleshooting Microsoft Windows

Chapter 10: Network Technologies

Chapter 11: Installing and Managing Network Connections

Chapter 12: Supporting Laptops and Portable Computing Devices

Chapter 13: Supporting Printers and Scanners

Chapter 14: Personal Computer Security Concepts

Chapter 15: Supporting Personal Computer Security

Glossary 371

About This Course

If you are getting ready for a career as an entry-level information technology (IT) professional or personal computer (PC) service technician, the *CompTIA® A+® Certification* course is the first step in your preparation. The course will build on your existing user-level knowledge and experience with personal computer software and hardware to present fundamental skills and concepts that you will use on the job. In this course, you will acquire the essential skills and information you will need to install, upgrade, repair, configure, troubleshoot, optimize, and perform preventative maintenance of basic personal computer hardware and operating systems.

The *CompTIA® A+® Certification* course can benefit you in two ways. Whether you work or plan to work in a mobile or corporate environment where you have a high level of face-to-face customer interaction, a remote-based environment where client interaction, client training, operating systems and connectivity issues are emphasized, or in an environment with limited customer interaction and an emphasis on hardware activities, this course provides the background knowledge and skills you will require to be successful. It can also assist you if you are preparing to take the CompTIA A+ certification examinations, 2006 objectives (exam numbers 220-601, 220-602, 220-603, and 220-604), in order to become a CompTIA A+ Certified Professional.

Course Description

Target Student

The target student is anyone with basic computer user skills who is interested in obtaining a job as an IT professional or PC technician. Possible job environments include mobile or corporate settings with a high level of face-to-face client interaction, remote-based work environments where client interaction, client training, operating systems, and connectivity issues are emphasized, or settings with limited customer interaction where hardware activities are emphasized. In addition, this course will help prepare students to achieve a CompTIA A+ Certification.

Course Prerequisites

Students taking this course should have the following skills:

- End-user skills with Windows-based personal computers, including the ability to:
  - Browse and search for information on the Internet.
  - Start up, shut down, and log on to a computer and network.
  - Run programs.
  - Move, copy, delete, and rename files in Windows Explorer.
- Basic knowledge of computing concepts, including the difference between hardware and software; the functions of software components, such as the operating system, applications, and file systems; and the function of a computer network.

How to Use This Book

As a Practice Guide

The *CompTIA® A+® Certification* lab guide is a companion to the *CompTIA® A+® Certification* textbook designed to give you the practical experience demonstrating, applying, and integrating the knowledge and skills you need to master *CompTIA® A+® Certification*.

All exercises and labs are designed to keep you actively involved in learning the content and help you transfer the skills you learn to your own situations. Exercise and labs are arranged in order of increasing proficiency: skills covered in one chapter are used and developed in subsequent chapters. You will notice a progression in your comprehension, application, and integration of skills throughout the course.

Certification

This course is designed to help you prepare for the following certification.

Certification Path: A+ Certification

- Exam: Essentials 220-601
- Exam: IT Technician 220-602
- Exam: Remote Technician 220-603
- Exam: Depot Technician 220-604

Course Objectives

In this course, you will install, upgrade, repair, configure, optimize, troubleshoot, and perform preventative maintenance on basic personal computer hardware and operating systems.

You will:

- identify the components of standard desktop personal computers.
- identify fundamental components and functions of personal computer operating systems.
- identify best practices followed by professional personal computer technicians.
- install and configure computer components.
- install and configure system components.
- maintain and troubleshoot peripheral components.
- troubleshoot system components.
- install and configure operating systems.
- maintain and troubleshoot installations of Microsoft Windows.
- identify network technologies.
- install and manage network connections.
- support laptops and portable computing devices.
- support printers and scanners.
- identify personal computer security concepts.
- support personal computer security.

Course Requirements

Hardware

Each student and the instructor will require one computer. The class is designed for each pair of students to work at a student lab station that should consist of one desktop computer, one laptop/portable computer, and one printer. If you do not have enough laptop computers to have one per lab station, provide as many as you can and provide the remaining students with desktop computers. If you do not have enough physical printers to have one per lab station, provide sufficient printers so that students can have adequate hands-on access to the printer mechanisms and components. You will also need to provide other hardware items for students to install; wherever possible provide enough components so that each lab station can install each device. The specifications for the desktop and laptop computers, as well as a list of other hardware items you will need to provide, follow.

- Desktop computers should be ATX-based systems with PCI slots. Additional bus types, such as ISA slots, are a plus. The system should also include the following ports: parallel, VGA, PS/2 keyboard port, PS/2 mouse port, serial, USB, and, if possible, sound ports including Line In, Line Out, Mic, and Game. Any additional ports are a plus. Desktop systems should have bootable CD-ROM drives and floppy drives.

- Portable computers should have a floppy drive and a CD/DVD drive (these can be swappable in a single drive bay, or separate components); at least one PC card slot; a mini-PCI card bay; and an empty memory slot.

- All computers should be 300 Mhz Pentium systems or higher.

- All computers should have 8 GB hard disks or larger.

- All computers should have 128 MB of RAM or more.

- All computers should have a keyboard and mouse.

- All computers should have a 800x600-capable display adapter and monitor.

- Laptop computers should have a docking station or port replicator to support the standard peripherals (keyboard, mouse, monitor).

- All computers should have network adapters and appropriate network cabling.

- Provide printing devices of your choice. You might wish to have different printer types, such as laser printers and inkjet printers, if available.

- The instructor's computer should have a projection system so the students can follow activities and demonstrations and so the instructor can display the course slide presentation.

- Provide two floppy disks for each student and the instructor.

- Each student should have a basic computer toolkit including an anti-static wrist strap, screwdrivers, tweezers and other small tools, and a multimeter. You may wish to provide other sample tools to the students, such as a power supply tester, as well as masking tape and pens. (Some of these items are included in the basic toolkit that is provided with the full courseware kit.)

- Each lab station should have a cleaning kit that includes monitor cleaning wipes, keyboard cleaning wipes, lint-free cloths, rubbing alcohol, cotton swabs, lens cloth, window cleaner, toothpicks, paint brush, compressed air canister, and computer vacuum.

- A classroom Internet connection.

- Each PC should contain the following internal devices that students can remove and reinstall, examine for troubleshooting purposes, or use to perform maintenance techniques: a hard disk; memory modules; power supply; one or more adapter cards; cooling systems.

- If the computers do not have integrated sound support, install sound cards.

- Provide a second, compatible hard drive and a cable that will enable a second hard drive to be added to student computers.

- Provide a multimedia device of some type for students to install.

- Provide the appropriate cabling for all devices.

- Provide as many other samples of different types of computer components as possible to display for the students. This can include adapter cards for various bus types, SCSI, PATA, and SATA storage devices, a variety of ports and cables, USB devices or hubs, multimedia devices such as digital cameras or microphones, gaming devices such as joysticks, various network cables and connectors, different display device types, different printer types, internal or external modems, examples of different motherboards, CPUs, and chipsets, and so on. Although you cannot work hands-on with every conceivable type of PC component within the confines of the classroom, the more different component types students can see and handle, the more beneficial their learning experience will be.

- Some activities and labs might require or suggest additional materials, so be sure to review the activity-specific setup requirements throughout the course prior to teaching this class.

Software

The following software is required for this course:

- Windows XP Professional with appropriate licenses. This will be installed during initial classroom setup, and students will install it again during class. Provide as many copies of the installation CD-ROM as possible. You might also wish to provide a separate classroom server computer, and copy the installation source files to a shared folder on the server.

- Windows XP Home with appropriate licenses. (If you prefer, you may substitute Windows 2000 Professional.) Students will install this operating system in class, so you should provide as many copies of the installation CD-ROM as possible. You might also wish to provide a separate classroom server computer, and copy the installation source files to a shared folder on the server.

- Classroom Internet access. Please configure Internet access and TCP/IP settings as appropriate for your classroom environment.

- Windows XP Professional Service Pack 2 or later and all current security patches. The setup instructions and classroom activities assume that you will obtain these through an Internet connection. Otherwise, you must download all current Windows XP Professional critical updates to installation CD-ROMs and have those available to the students to complete operating system setup.

- Device drivers and software manuals for each device the students will install. You should be able to obtain this live from the Internet during class; if not, you can download the drivers and burn them to a CD-ROM or place them on a network share, or provide the manufacturers' original disks.

Class Setup

For Instructor and Student Desktop and Laptop Operating System Installation:

1. Make sure that all computer components are properly installed and working.

2. Perform a fresh installation of Windows XP Professional. You can boot the computer from the installation CD-ROM, or create a network boot disk and install from a network share. After you configure the first computer of each type, you might wish to create a ghost image and install that to the remaining classroom computers. Regardless of your installation method, use the following installation parameters:

   - Accept the license agreement.

   - Delete existing partitions.

   - Create a 6 GB NTFS C partition. When you do this, make sure that you leave at least 2 GB of free space.

   - Select the appropriate regional settings for your location.

   - Enter the appropriate user name and organization for your environment.

   - Enter the product key.

- For the instructor's computer, use a computer name of INST. For each of the student computers, use a computer name of CLIENT##, where ## is a unique two-digit number assigned to each student.

- Set the default administrator account password to !Pass1234.

- Configure the appropriate date and time for your location.

- Accept the Typical network settings; or, if necessary, configure Custom settings as appropriate to support Internet access or to conform to the network configuration of your classroom environment.

- Install the computer into the default workgroup.

- After the computer restarts, if prompted to turn on Automatic Updates, select Not Right Now. Then, complete the Internet connection portion as appropriate for your environment. If the computer will connect via a LAN connection, you should be able to skip this portion.

- Complete the system activation portion as appropriate for your environment. Training centers are responsible for complying with all relevant Microsoft licensing and activation requirements.

- On the Who Will Use This Computer screen, in the Your Name text box, enter a user account named Admin##, where ## matches the number in the computer name. At the instructor computer, name the account simply Admin. This account will become a member of the local Administrators group by default.

When setup is complete, the system will automatically log you on as Admin## with a blank password.

3. Set the Admin## account password.

   a. From the Start menu, click Control Panel, click User Accounts, and then click the Admin## account.

   b. Click Create a Password.

   c. Enter and confirm !Pass1234 as the password, and then click Create Password.

   d. Click Yes, Make Private and close all open windows.

4. If Service Pack 2 is not slipstreamed into your Windows XP Professional installation media, and you have a Service Pack 2 installation CD-ROM, install Service Pack 2 manually.

5. Choose Start→All Programs→Windows Update. From the Windows Update website, download and install all High Priority updates, including any current service packs and recommended security patches.

6. Configure workgroup networking so that all classroom computers can connect to each other.

   a. From the Start menu, open My Computer→My Network Places.

   b. Click Set Up A Home Or Small Office Network.

   c. In the Network Setup Wizard, click Next twice.

   d. On the Select a Connection Method screen, select Other and click Next.

   e. On the Other Internet Connection Methods screen, select This Computer Belongs To A Network That Does Not Have An Internet Connection and click Next.

   f. Accept the computer name by clicking Next.

   g. On the Name Your Network screen, enter WORKGROUP as the workgroup name and click Next twice.

h.   If prompted, turn on File And Printer Sharing and click Next. Review the parameters and click Next.

i.   On the You're Almost Done screen, select Just Finish The Wizard, click Next, and then click Finish.

7.   Use the Start→Run command or My Network Places to verify that all classroom computers can connect without entering a user name or password.

8.   To install the course data files, insert the course CD-ROM and click the Data Files button. This will install a folder named 085820Data on your C drive. This folder contains all the data files that you will use to complete this course. It also includes several simulated activities that can be used in lieu of the hands-on activities in the course.

9.   Close all open windows and log out.

For Individual Labs and Activities

Prior to teaching the class, review the Setup instructions for the individual labs and activities throughout the course for additional activity-specific equipment requirements and setup procedures.

List of Additional Files

Printed with each activity is a list of files students open to complete that activity. Many activities also require additional files that students do not open, but are needed to support the file(s) students are working with. These supporting files are included with the student data files on the course CD-ROM or data disk. Do not delete these files.

1 | Personal Computer Components

Activities included in this chapter:

- Exercise 1-1 Identifying Personal Computer Components
- Exercise 1-2 Identifying System Unit Components
- Exercise 1-3 Identifying Storage Devices
- Exercise 1-4 Identifying Personal Computer Connection Methods
- Lab 1-1 Identifying Personal Computer Components

EXERCISE 1-1

Identifying Personal Computer Components

Scenario:
In this activity, you will identify personal computer components.

1. **Identify the computer components in the graphic.**

___	A	a. Display device
___	B	b. External device
___	C	c. Input device
___	D	d. System unit

2. **Which computer components are part of the system unit?**

    a) Chassis

    b) Monitor

    c) Internal hard drive

    d) Portable USB drive

    e) Memory

3. **Match each external device with its function.**

___	Microphone	a. Provides audio output.
___	Speaker	b. Provides graphical input.
___	Scanner	c. Provides text and graphical output.
___	Printer	d. Provides audio input.
___	External drive	e. Provides additional data storage.

Check Your Knowledge

1. What are two of the most common input devices you may encounter in any desktop computer setup?

   _____

   _____

2. List some of the common components you will find in a computer's system unit.

   _____

   _____

3. List some of the common external components you will find in a desktop computer setup.

   _____

   _____

EXERCISE 1-2

Identifying System Unit Components

Scenario:

In this activity, you will identify system unit components.

1. **Identify the system unit components in this graphic.**

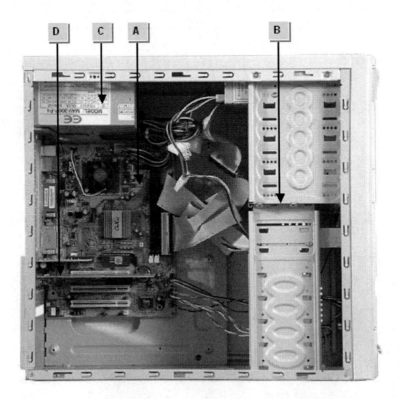

___	A	a. Storage device
___	B	b. Power supply
___	C	c. System board
___	D	d. Adapter card

2. **Identify the system unit components shown in this graphic.**

___	A	a.	Memory
___	B	b.	CPU

3. **What is a system bus?**

   a) The communication path from memory to the adapter card slots.

   b) The communication path between the CPU and memory.

   c) The connection between the power supply and the system board.

   d) The electronic pathway between the CPU and the storage devices.

4. **True or False? There is at least one cooling system inside almost every personal computer.**

   ___ True

   ___ False

Check Your Knowledge

1. Where would you typically find fans and heatsinks being used to cool a system component?

   _____

   _____

   _____

2. What are some of the physical characteristics of system board slots that allow you to identify their use?

   _____

   _____

   _____

EXERCISE 1-3

Identifying Storage Devices

Scenario:
In this activity, you will identify storage devices.

---

1. **Match the storage type with the appropriate description.**

___	Floppy disk drive	a.	Records data magnetically; most often used for backups.
___	Hard disk drive	b.	Records and reads data by using a laser.
___	Optical disk drive	c.	Records data magnetically on removable disks.
___	Tape drive	d.	Records data on non-removable disks.
___	Solid state storage	e.	Records data in memory that emulates a mechanical storage device.

2. **Which optical drive media types enable you to write to an optical disk only once?**

   a) CD-ROM

   b) CD-R

   c) CD-RW

   d) DVD-R

   e) DVD-RW

Check Your Knowledge

1. Which optical media types allow you to reuse the media more than once?

   _____

2. Which storage devices record data magnetically?

   _____

EXERCISE 1-4

Identifying Personal Computer Connection Methods

Scenario:

In this activity, you will identify personal computer connection methods.

1. **Identify the connection types listed.**

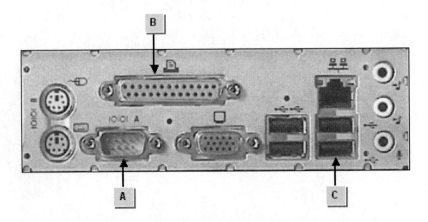

___   A   a.   Parallel

___   B   b.   Serial

___   C   c.   USB

2. **Which PC connection type is sometimes called IDE?**

   a) FireWire

   b) PATA

   c) SATA

   d) SCSI

   e) USB

3. **Which connection type supports up to 127 peripherals in a single connection?**

   a) IEEE 1394

   b) SATA

   c) Parallel

   d) USB

4. **Which cable has the smallest connectors?**

    a) SCSI

    b) PATA

    c) SATA

    d) Parallel

Check Your Knowledge

1. Which connection type is also known as IEEE 1394?

    _____

2. When identifying ports on the back of a computer, what are some visual characteristics you can use to more easily identify their purpose?

    _____

    _____

    _____

    _____

    _____

3. Which technologies does PATA encompass?

    _____

LAB 1-1

Identifying Personal Computer Components

Activity Time: 10 minutes

Scenario:

1. **What are the main categories of personal computer components?**

   a) System unit

   b) Display device

   c) Input devices

   d) Network devices

   e) External devices

2. **Which system unit components are connected by the system bus?**

   a) CPU

   b) Memory

   c) Power supply

   d) System board

   e) Cooling system

3. **Which storage device uses special memory to store data?**

   a) Floppy disk drive

   b) Hard disk drive

   c) Optical drive

   d) Tape drive

   e) Solid state storage

4. **Match the connection type with its most common use.**

___	Serial connection	a. Connecting a modem.
___	Parallel connection	b. Connecting a peripheral device with a cable that has Type A and Type B connectors.
___	USB connection	c. Connecting a peripheral device with a cable that has square or bullet-shaped connectors.
___	FireWire	d. Connecting a series of hard disk drives in a master/slave configuration.
___	SCSI	e. Connecting a hard disk drive with a 4-pin connector.
___	PATA	f. Connecting a high-speed hard disk drive.
___	SATA	g. Connecting a printer.

5. **Examine as many different personal computer systems as you can. Locate the four primary components of each system, and determine what types of input devices, output devices, and external devices each uses. Is the system unit desktop-style, tower-style, or is it some kind of portable system? Identify the ports available on the computer. See if you can tell which ports are built in and which are provided by adapter cards. Try to determine what types of internal storage devices each system provides.**

2 | Operating System Fundamentals

Activities included in this chapter:

- Exercise 2-1 Discussing Operating Systems
- Exercise 2-2 Examining the Taskbar and Start Menu
- Exercise 2-3 Examining Folder Management Tools
- Exercise 2-4 Exploring the Control Panel
- Exercise 2-5 Running the Command Prompt
- Exercise 2-6 Exploring My Network Places
- Exercise 2-7 Viewing File Extensions
- Exercise 2-8 Exploring File Attributes
- Exercise 2-9 Exploring NTFS Permissions
- Exercise 2-10 Examining Computer Management
- Exercise 2-11 Examining the Structure of the Registry
- Lab 2-1 Configuring Windows Operating System Components

EXERCISE 2-1

Discussing Operating Systems

Scenario:

In this activity, you will discuss various personal computer operating systems.

1. **Match the version of Windows with its description.**

___	Windows XP Professional	a. A desktop version of Windows that provided a graphical shell for DOS.
___	Windows XP Home	b. The flagship Windows version intended for desktop use in corporate business environments as well as for general use.
___	Windows XP Media Center	c. A version of Windows that is optimized for activities such as recording live TV, playing music, and managing digital images.
___	Windows 98	d. A popular complete Windows operating system including network support, built on a unique code base that is no longer supported.
___	Windows 3.1	e. A version of Windows intended for private users, with a limited set of security and management features.
___	Windows 2000 Professional	f. A desktop version, no longer supported, of Microsoft's enterprise server operating system software.

2. **Which statements about UNIX are true?**

   a) There are many versions of UNIX from different developers and distributors.

   b) All versions of UNIX use the same shell, or user interface.

   c) UNIX versions are proprietary.

   d) UNIX is a multiuser, multitasking system.

   e) It was developed using open-source methodology.

3. **Which statements about Linux are true?**

   a) It was developed as open-source software.

   b) Developers must obtain permission to access and modify the source code.

   c) Development was initiated and managed by Linus Torvalds.

   d) Releases of Linux are unstable.

   e) Linux distributions can provide tools, utilities, and system support.

4. **Mac OS X can:**

    a) Be downloaded and modified freely.

    b) Integrate browsing for files created in other operating systems.

    c) Support many hardware devices.

    d) Run the Windows XP user interface.

Check Your Knowledge

1. Which version of Windows XP is better suited for use in a PC to be used as part of a home entertainment center?

2. Which operating systems are better suited for large scale servers?

3. Which version of Windows XP can be used both at home and in a business environment without compromising any features?

EXERCISE 2-2

Examining the Taskbar and Start Menu

Scenario:
In this activity, you will examine the Windows XP taskbar and Start menu.

 There is a simulated version of this activity available on the CD-ROM that shipped with this course. You can run this simulation on any Windows computer to review the activity after class, or as an alternative to performing the activity as a group in class. The activity simulation can be launched either directly from the CD-ROM by clicking the Interactives link and navigating to the appropriate one, or from the installed data file location by opening the C:\085820Data\Simulations\Lesson#\Activity# folder and double-clicking the executable (.exe) file.

What You Do	How You Do It
1. **Log on to Windows XP Professional.**	a. On the Welcome Screen, **click the Admin## user account.**
	b. In the Type Your Password text box, **type !Pass1234 and press Enter.**
2. **Examine the Start menu.**	a. **Click the Start menu.**
	b. The name of the current user appears at the top of the Start menu. There are areas for pinned programs, frequently-used programs, and links to applications, folders, and menus. **Point to the All Programs menu.**
	c. The All Programs menu contains several submenus. To run a program and close the Start menu, **choose Accessories→ Notepad.**

3.   Identify the areas of the taskbar.

a.   Buttons on the taskbar enable you to access running programs and open documents. To minimize Notepad, **click the Notepad button on the taskbar.**

b.   To close Notepad from the taskbar, **right-click the Notepad button and choose Close.**

c.   The system tray at the right end of the taskbar contains links to system accessories. You can point to the current time in the system tray to display the date and time. **Double-click the current time in the system tray** to open the Clock program.

d.   Administrators can use the Date And Time Properties box to change the date, time, and time zone. **Click OK.**

e.   **Right-click an open area of the taskbar and choose Toolbars→Quick Launch.**

f.   The Quick Launch toolbar provides one-click access to frequently-used programs. In the Quick Launch toolbar, **click the Internet Explorer icon.**

g.   **Close the Internet Explorer window.**

4. **Examine the Start menu and taskbar configuration settings.**

a. **Right-click an open area of the taskbar and choose Properties.**

b. You can make various selections to affect the appearance and behavior of the taskbar and notification area. **Click the Start Menu tab.**

c. You can choose the Start Menu or Classic Start Menu display, and you can customize either one. **Click OK.**

Check Your Knowledge

1. On the Start menu, where are frequently used programs displayed?

   _____

2. How can a user quickly launch an application without having to access it through the Start menu or through a shortcut on the desktop?

   _____

   _____

3. Why would it be necessary to change the Start menu to the Classic Start menu?

   _____

   _____

   _____

EXERCISE 2-3

Examining Folder Management Tools

Scenario:

In this activity, you will examine the My Documents folder and other contents of My Computer and Windows Explorer.

 There is a simulated version of this activity available on the CD-ROM that shipped with this course. You can run this simulation on any Windows computer to review the activity after class, or as an alternative to performing the activity as a group in class. The activity simulation can be launched either directly from the CD-ROM by clicking the Interactives link and navigating to the appropriate one, or from the installed data file location by opening the C:\ 085820Data\Simulations\Lesson#\Activity# folder and double-clicking the executable (.exe) file.

What You Do	How You Do It
1. **Examine My Computer.**	a. **Choose Start→My Computer.**
	b. The My Computer window has a blue Task Pane on the left. The window shows the various drives, folders, and other storage areas available on the computer. To open drive C, **double-click the Local Disk (C:) icon.**
	c. You can see the folders on the C drive. The contents of the Task Pane change according to the contents of the folder window. In the Task Pane, under Other Places, **click My Computer.**
	d. The Address bar provides another way to navigate the contents of My Computer. In the Address bar, **click the drop-down arrow.**
	e. In the Address list, **click Local Disk (C:).**
	f. To return to the My Computer view, **click the Address drop-down arrow and choose My Computer.**

2. **Examine My Documents.**

a. In the Task Pane, under Other Places, **click My Documents.**

b. By default, the My Documents folder contains two subfolders, My Music and My Pictures. **Click the My Computer link.**

c. The My Documents folder for the current user appears in My Computer. **Double-click the Admin##'s Documents folder icon.**

d. **Close the My Documents window.**

e. My Documents is also available from the Start menu. **Choose Start→My Documents.**

f. **Close the My Documents window.**

3.   **Examine Windows Explorer.**

a.   **Choose Start→All Programs→ Accessories→Windows Explorer.**

b.   Windows Explorer has a two-pane view that shows the Explorer bar on the left and the folder contents on the right. In the Explorer bar, in the Folders list, **click the plus signs to expand My Computer, Local Disk (C:).**

c.   You can see the folder hierarchy for drive C. To see the contents of drive C, **select Local Disk (C:).**

d.   To close the Folders list and switch to My Computer view, **click the Close box in the Explorer Bar.**

e.   To switch back to Windows Explorer view, **choose View→Explorer Bar→Folders.**

f.   **Close Windows Explorer.**

g.   You can use the Explore choice to open an Explorer view of any selected item. **Choose Start, right-click My Documents, and choose Explore.**

h.   **Close Windows Explorer.**

Check Your Knowledge

1.   In which folder are user files stored by default?

_____

_____

2.   What is the purpose of Windows Explorer?

_____

_____

3.   What is the advantage of using Windows Explorer's two-pane view?

_____

_____

EXERCISE 2-4

Exploring the Control Panel

Scenario:

In this activity, you will explore the components of the Control Panel.

 There is a simulated version of this activity available on the CD-ROM that shipped with this course. You can run this simulation on any Windows computer to review the activity after class, or as an alternative to performing the activity as a group in class. The activity simulation can be launched either directly from the CD-ROM by clicking the Interactives link and navigating to the appropriate one, or from the installed data file location by opening the C:\085820Data\Simulations\Lesson#\Activity# folder and double-clicking the executable (.exe) file.

What You Do	How You Do It
1. Examine Control Panel utilities.	a. **Choose Start→Control Panel.**
	b. Control Panel tools are grouped by function. **Click Appearance And Themes.**
	c. Appearance And Themes contains a number of related tools and links, as well as context-sensitive links in the Task Pane. **Click Taskbar And Start Menu.**
	d. The Taskbar And Start Menu Properties dialog box opens. **Click Cancel.**
	e. **Click the Back button.**
	f. **Examine other categories in Control Panel.**

2. Change the Control Panel view.

a. In the Task Pane, **click Switch To Classic View.**

b. **Click Switch To Category View.**

c. You might see either one of these views on Windows XP computers. **Close Control Panel.**

Check Your Knowledge

1. What is the difference between Category view and Classic view in Control Panel?

_____

_____

2. When in Category view, what other information is displayed in Control Panel?

_____

EXERCISE 2-5

Running the Command Prompt

Scenario:

In this activity, you will run the Command Prompt interface and enter basic commands.

 There is a simulated version of this activity available on the CD-ROM that shipped with this course. You can run this simulation on any Windows computer to review the activity after class, or as an alternative to performing the activity as a group in class. The activity simulation can be launched either directly from the CD-ROM by clicking the Interactives link and navigating to the appropriate one, or from the installed data file location by opening the C:\085820Data\Simulations\Lesson#\Activity# folder and double-clicking the executable (.exe) file.

What You Do	How You Do It
1. **Open a Command Prompt.**	a. **Choose Start→All Programs→ Accessories→Command Prompt.**
	b. The default path for the prompt is the user profile folder for the current user (C:\ Documents and Settings*username*). **Maximize the Command Prompt window.**
2. **Enter commands at the prompt.**	a. To display the current operating system version, **enter *ver***
	b. To change to the root of the current drive, **enter *cd ***
	c. To see the contents of the current folder, **enter *dir***
3. **Create a folder.**	a. At the C:\> prompt, **enter *md LocalData* and press Enter.**

b. To verify that the folder was created, **enter dir**

```
C:\>md LocalData

C:\>dir
 Volume in drive C has no label.
 Volume Serial Number is E4AD-D8A1

 Directory of C:\

03/23/2006  11:48 AM    <DIR>          Apps
01/21/2005  01:45 PM    <DIR>          Compaq
01/21/2005  01:43 PM    <DIR>          cpqs
09/26/2006  03:24 PM    <DIR>          Documents and Settings
09/27/2006  10:18 AM    <DIR>          General
01/21/2005  01:42 PM    <DIR>          i386
09/27/2006  12:38 PM    <DIR>          LocalData
01/21/2005  11:27 AM    <DIR>          Program Files
09/26/2006  03:53 PM    <DIR>          WINDOWS
               0 File(s)              0 bytes
               9 Dir(s)  34,431,594,496 bytes free

C:\>_
```

c. To close the Command Prompt window, **enter the command** *exit*

Check Your Knowledge

1. When at the Command Prompt, which command would the user enter to obtain the operating system version?

2. List the basic commands that allow the user to navigate a directory tree while in the Command Prompt.

EXERCISE 2-6

Exploring My Network Places

Scenario:

In this activity, you will explore the My Network Places interface.

 There is a simulated version of this activity available on the CD-ROM that shipped with this course. You can run this simulation on any Windows computer to review the activity after class, or as an alternative to performing the activity as a group in class. The activity simulation can be launched either directly from the CD-ROM by clicking the Interactives link and navigating to the appropriate one, or from the installed data file location by opening the C:\ 085820Data\Simulations\Lesson#\Activity# folder and double-clicking the executable (.exe) file.

What You Do	How You Do It
1. **Examine Network Places.**	a. **Choose Start→My Network Places.**
	b. The Task Pane shows network-related tasks; the window shows any Network Places shortcuts the system has created. **Click View Workgroup Computers.**
	c. You can see the computers in your workgroup, including your computer. **Double-click one of the workgroup computers.**
	d. You can see shared resources on the selected computer. **Click the Address drop-down arrow and choose Microsoft Windows Network.**
	e. The Microsoft Windows Network view enables you to see all workgroups on your local network, including your own. To return to My Network Places, **click the Address drop-down arrow and choose My Network Places.**

2. **Examine the Add A Network Place function.**

   a. In the Task Pane, **click Add A Network Place.**

   b. **Click Next.**

   c. **Verify that Choose Another Network Location is selectedmm, and click Next.**

   d. To see some examples of network place shortcut addresses, click **View Some Examples.**

   Examples:
   \\server\share (shared folder)
   http://webserver/share (Web Share)
   ftp://ftp.microsoft.com (FTP site)

   e. **Click the Examples speech bubble** to close it.

   f. **Click Cancel.**

   g. **Close My Network Places.**

Check Your Knowledge

1. How can the user browse other workgroups available on the network?

   _____

   _____

2. How can the user browse all computers available in his or her workgroup?

   _____

   _____

   _____

3. Once a network resource is identified, how can a user save its location to avoid having to search for it the next time it is needed?

   _____

   _____

EXERCISE 2-7

Viewing File Extensions

Scenario:
In this activity, you will view the file extensions of default files on your Windows system.

 There is a simulated version of this activity available on the CD-ROM that shipped with this course. You can run this simulation on any Windows computer to review the activity after class, or as an alternative to performing the activity as a group in class. The activity simulation can be launched either directly from the CD-ROM by clicking the Interactives link and navigating to the appropriate one, or from the installed data file location by opening the C:\ 085820Data\Simulations\Lesson#\Activity# folder and double-clicking the executable (.exe) file.

What You Do	How You Do It
1. **Open the folder containing the Windows system files.**	a. **Choose Start→My Computer.**
	b. **Double-click the C drive.**
	c. **Double-click the Windows folder.**
	d. Because this is a system folder, the contents do not automatically display. **Click Show The Contents Of This Folder.**

2. **Display the file extensions.**

    a. **Choose Tools→Folder Options.**

    b. **Click the View tab.**

    c. **Uncheck Hide Extensions For Known File Types and click OK.**

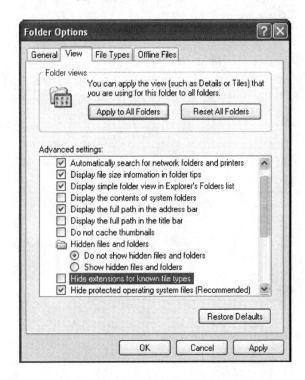

3. **Examine the file extensions.**

    a. The first few files in the window have a number of different extensions. To see all the files in a list, **choose View→List.**

    b. To see similar extensions grouped together, **choose View→Arrange Icons By→Type.**

    c. To return to the default view, **choose View→Arrange Icons By→Name.**

4. **Match the Windows file name with its file type, based on its extension.**

    ___ Notepad.exe   a. Configuration settings.

    ___ Setuplog.txt   b. A graphics file.

    ___ Coffee Bean.bmp   c. An application file.

    ___ System.ini   d. A document containing text but no formatting.

    ___ Twain.dll   e. A file that contains supporting functionality for applications.

Check Your Knowledge

1. In which directory are Windows XP system files stored?

   _____

2. File extensions are hidden by default in Windows XP. How can you display file extensions?

   _____
   _____
   _____

EXERCISE 2-8

Exploring File Attributes

Setup:
The C:\Windows folder is open in My Computer. There is a C:\LocalData folder on the system.

Scenario:
In this activity, you will explore the attribute settings on a data file.

 There is a simulated version of this activity available on the CD-ROM that shipped with this course. You can run this simulation on any Windows computer to review the activity after class, or as an alternative to performing the activity as a group in class. The activity simulation can be launched either directly from the CD-ROM by clicking the Interactives link and navigating to the appropriate one, or from the installed data file location by opening the C:\ 085820Data\Simulations\Lesson#\Activity# folder and double-clicking the executable (.exe) file.

What You Do	How You Do It
1. **Create a new data file.**	a. In My Computer, **click the Address drop-down arrow and choose C:\.**
	b. **Double-click the LocalData folder.**
	c. **Choose File→New→Text Document.**
	d. To accept the default file name, **press Enter.**

2.	**View the basic attributes of a text file.**	a.	In the Windows Explorer window, with the New Text Document.txt file selected, **choose File→Properties.**
		b.	You can set the Read-only and Hidden attributes on the General page. **Click Advanced.**
		c.	You can set the Archive and Index attributes in the Advanced Attributes dialog box. **Click Cancel twice.**
3.	**View attributes from the command line.**	a.	**Open a Command Prompt window.**
		b.	To change to the LocalData folder, **enter** *cd \localdata*
		c.	To view the current attributes of the file, **enter** *attrib*
		d.	To add the System attribute, **enter** *attrib +s*
		e.	To view the current attributes of the file, **enter** *attrib*

```
Microsoft Windows XP [Version 5.1.2600]
(C) Copyright 1985-2001 Microsoft Corp.

C:\Documents and Settings\Admin04>cd \localdata

C:\LocalData>attrib
A          C:\LocalData\New Text Document.txt

C:\LocalData>attrib +s

C:\LocalData>attrib
A   S      C:\LocalData\New Text Document.txt

C:\LocalData>_
```

| | | f. | To remove the System attribute, **enter** *attrib -s* |
| | | g. | To close the Command Prompt window, **click the Close button.** ☒ |

Check Your Knowledge

1. What is the quickest way of creating a blank text file?

   _____

   _____

2. What kind of information can be obtained when you view a file's properties?

   _____

   _____

   _____

3. When changing a file's attributes using the command line, which switches are used with the attrib command to make a file both system and read-only?

   _____

   _____

EXERCISE 2-9

Exploring NTFS Permissions

Setup:
The C:\LocalData folder is open in a My Computer window.

Scenario:
In this activity, you will examine NTFS file and folder permissions.

 There is a simulated version of this activity available on the CD-ROM that shipped with this course. You can run this simulation on any Windows computer to review the activity after class, or as an alternative to performing the activity as a group in class. The activity simulation can be launched either directly from the CD-ROM by clicking the Interactives link and navigating to the appropriate one, or from the installed data file location by opening the C:\085820Data\Simulations\Lesson#\Activity# folder and double-clicking the executable (.exe) file.

What You Do	How You Do It
1. Turn off Simple File Sharing.	a. In the C:\LocalData folder window, **choose Tools→Folder Options.**
	b. **Click the View tab.**
	c. **Scroll to the bottom of the Advanced Settings list.**
	d. **Uncheck Use Simple File Sharing (Recommended) and click OK.**
2. Examine NTFS permissions on a drive.	a. To move to My Computer, on the toolbar, **click the Up icon twice.**
	b. **Select the C drive and choose File→ Properties.**
	c. **Click the Security tab.**

d. In the Group Or User Names list, the Administrators group should be selected. **Determine the permissions assigned to the Administrators group.**

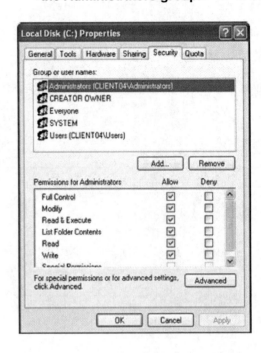

e. **Select the Users group.**

f. **Determine the permissions assigned to the Users group and click Cancel.**

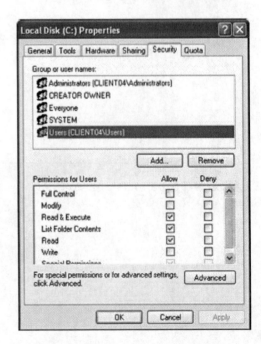

3. **What level of permissions did the Administrators group have?**

    a) Full Control

    b) Modify

    c) Write

    d) Read & Execute

4. **What level of permissions did the Users group have?**

    a) Full Control

    b) Modify

    c) Write

    d) Read & Execute

5. **Examine NTFS folder permissions.**

    a. **Double-click the C drive.**

    b. **Select the LocalData folder and choose File→Properties.**

    c. **Click the Security tab.**

    d. **Select the Administrators group.**

    e. **Determine the permissions assigned to the Administrators group.**

    f. **Select the Users group.**

    g. **Determine the permissions assigned to the Users group and click Cancel.**

6. **How were the permissions on the LocalData folder different from the permissions on the C drive?**

    a) Administrators did not have Full Control to the LocalData folder.

    b) Users could not read files in the LocalData folder.

    c) The permissions on the C drive were set explicitly; the permissions on the LocalData folder were inherited from the C drive.

    d) The available permissions were different.

7. Examine NTFS file permissions.	**a. Double-click the LocalData folder.**
	b. Select the New Text Document.txt file and choose File→Properties.
	c. Click the Security tab.
	d. Select the Administrators group.
	e. Determine the permissions assigned to the Administrators group.
	f. Select the Users group.
	g. Determine the permissions assigned to the Users group and click Cancel.
	h. Close the window.

8. True or False? The permissions on the New Text Document.txt file were inherited from the LocalData folder permissions.

___ True

___ False

Check Your Knowledge

1. How can you turn off Simple File Sharing in Windows XP Home?

2. How can you browse a user group's permissions?

3. When a new file is created, where are the file's permissions inherited from?

4. By default, the Administrators group has Full Control permissions, with all options selected. What are the default permissions for the Users group?

EXERCISE 2-10

Examining Computer Management

Scenario:

In this activity, you will explore the Computer Management utility.

 There is a simulated version of this activity available on the CD-ROM that shipped with this course. You can run this simulation on any Windows computer to review the activity after class, or as an alternative to performing the activity as a group in class. The activity simulation can be launched either directly from the CD-ROM by clicking the Interactives link and navigating to the appropriate one, or from the installed data file location by opening the C:\085820Data\Simulations\Lesson#\Activity# folder and double-clicking the executable (.exe) file.

What You Do	How You Do It
1. **Open Computer Management.**	a. You can open Computer Management from Control Panel or from the Start menu. **Choose Start, right-click My Computer, and choose Manage.**
	b. **Maximize the Computer Management window.**

2. **Examine the System Tools.**

   a. To view the categories of log files Windows maintains, **select Event Viewer.**

   b. To view the contents of a log file, **double-click System.**

   c. To view tools for managing shared network folders, **select Shared Folders.**

   d. To see the shared folders on the system, **double-click Shares.**

   e. To view tools for managing local computer accounts, **select Local Users And Groups.**

   f. To see the local users on the system, **double-click Users.**

   g. To view tools for logging performance data, **select Performance Logs And Alerts.**

   h. To view the status of devices attached to the system, **select Device Manager.**

3. **Examine the Storage node.**

   a. To examine tools for managing removable storage devices such as CD-ROMs, **select the Removable Storage node.**

   b. To examine the tool for defragmenting hard disks, **select Disk Defragmenter.**

   c. To examine the tool for managing physical disks, **select Disk Management.**

4. **Examine the Services And Applications node.**

   a. **Expand Services And Applications.**

   b. To see a list of available Windows services, **select Services.**

c. To see configuration settings for the WMI Control, **select WMI Control, then right-click and choose Properties.**

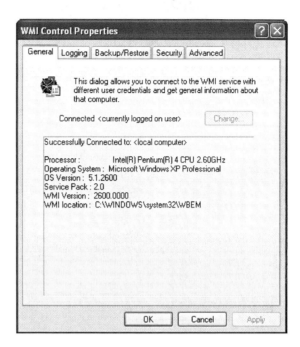

d. **Click Cancel.**

e. To see configuration tools that enable you to create a searchable index of files' contents, **select Indexing Service.**

f. There is a default catalog called System, but indexing is not active. **Close Computer Management.**

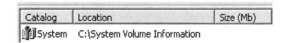

Check Your Knowledge

1. When managing a computer using the Computer Management control panel, what are some of the features you have available?

_____

_____

_____

_____

EXERCISE 2-11

Examining the Structure of the Registry

Scenario:
In this activity, you will examine the structure of the Windows registry.

 There is a simulated version of this activity available on the CD-ROM that shipped with this course. You can run this simulation on any Windows computer to review the activity after class, or as an alternative to performing the activity as a group in class. The activity simulation can be launched either directly from the CD-ROM by clicking the Interactives link and navigating to the appropriate one, or from the installed data file location by opening the C:\085820Data\Simulations\Lesson#\Activity# folder and double-clicking the executable (.exe) file.

What You Do	How You Do It
1. Run the Registry Editor.	a. **Choose Start→Run.**
	b. To run Registry Editor, in the Open text box, **type *regedit* and click OK.**
	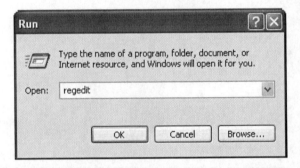
	c. **Maximize the Registry Editor window.**
2. Examine trees, keys, and value entries. 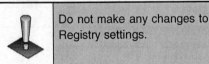Do not make any changes to Registry settings.	a. **Click the plus sign to expand HKEY_CURRENT_USER.**
	b. This tree contains all the settings that related to the currently-logged-on user. **Expand the Control Panel key.**

c. **Select the Desktop key.**

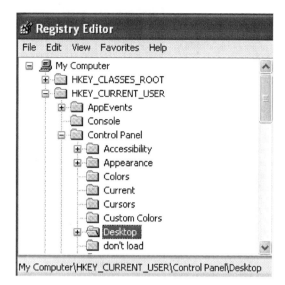

d. The value entries in this key determine the appearance and settings of the current user's Windows desktop. **Identify the components of several value entries.**

e. **Explore other areas of the Registry but be careful not to make any changes.**

f. **Close the Registry window.**

3. **Locate the Registry hive files.**

a. **Choose Start→My Computer.**

b. **Open the C drive.**

c. **Open the Windows folder.**

d. **Open the system32 folder.**

e. **Click Show The Contents Of This Folder.**

f. **Open the config folder.**

g. **Identify the Registry files (Default, SAM, Security, Software, and System), and close the window.**

Check Your Knowledge

1. What is the command you need to execute to open the Windows Registry Editor?

   _____

   _____

2. List the types of items you will see when accessing the Windows Registry using the Registry Editor.

   _____

3. Where are the Registry hive files stored?

   _____

LAB 2-1

Configuring Windows Operating System Components

Activity Time: 30 minutes

Scenario:

 You can find a suggested solution for this activity in the \Solutions\Configuring Windows Operating System Components.txt file in the data file location.

1. Configure the Start menu and taskbar settings that you prefer.

2. Configure the My Computer view and folder options that you prefer.

3. Create a data folder within My Documents and determine the default permissions and attributes on it.

4. Examine the tools available in the various categories within Control Panel.

5. Use the Windows Help And Support system to search for information about the tools available in Computer Management.

6. **Examine the information contained in various Registry trees, keys, and value entries.**

For example:

- In the HKEY_CURRENT_USER\Contol Panel\Current key, determine the value of Color Schemes. This will tell you which color scheme is in use.

- In the HKEY_CURRENT_USER\Control Panel\Mouse key, determine the value of SwapMouseButtons. This will be set to 0 if the left mouse button is configured as the primary button.

- In the HKEY_CLASSES_ROOT\txtfile\shell\open\command key, determine the value of the (default) value entry. This will tell you what application Windows will use by default to open files with an extension of .txt.

- In the HKEY_LOCAL_MACHINE\SOFTWARE\Microsoft\Windows\CurrentVersion key, determine the value of ProgramFilesDir. This will tell you in which folder Windows will install new software programs by default.

 Do not make any changes to the Registry.

3 | PC Technician Professional Best Practices

Activities included in this chapter:

- Exercise 3-1 Identifying Hardware and Software Tools
- Exercise 3-2 Identifying Electrical Safety Issues
- Exercise 3-3 Identifying Environmental Safety Issues
- Exercise 3-4 Performing Preventative Maintenance
- Exercise 3-5 Using a UPS
- Exercise 3-6 Identifying Troubleshooting Best Practices
- Exercise 3-7 Identifying Communication and Professionalism Best Practices
- Lab 3-1 Identifying PC Technician Professional Best Practices

EXERCISE 3-1

Identifying Hardware and Software Tools

Scenario:

In this activity, you will identify hardware and software tools commonly used by PC technicians.

---

1. **You've been asked to repair a system board in a customer's PC. Which set of tools would be best suited for the task?**

   a) Phillips screwdriver (#0), torx driver (size T15), tweezers, and a three-prong retriever.

   b) 30w ceramic solder iron, miniature pliers, wire cutters, and a solder iron stand with sponge.

   c) Wire strippers, precision wire cutters, digital multimeter, and cable crimper with dies.

   d) Chip extractor, chip inserter, rachet, and allen wrench.

   e) Anti-static cleaning wipes, anti-static wrist band, flashlight, and cotton swabs.

---

2. **You've been asked to correct a network cabling problem at a customer site. Which set of tools would be best suited for the task?**

   a) Phillips screwdriver (#0), torx driver (size T15), tweezers, and a three-prong retriever.

   b) 30w ceramic solder iron, miniature pliers, wire cutters, and a solder iron stand with sponge.

   c) Wire strippers, precision wire cutters, digital multimeter, and cable crimper with dies.

   d) Chip extractor, chip inserter, rachet, and allen wrench.

   e) Anti-static cleaning wipes, anti-static wrist band, flashlight, and cotton swabs.

---

3. **You suspect that contaminants from the environment have prevented the fan on a PC from working optimally. Which set of tools would be best suited to fix the problem?**

   a) Phillips screwdriver (#0), torx driver (size T15), tweezers, and a three-prong retriever.

   b) 30w ceramic solder iron, miniature pliers, wire cutters, and a solder iron stand with sponge.

   c) Wire strippers, precision wire cutters, digital multimeter, and cable crimper with dies.

   d) Chip extractor, chip inserter, rachet, and allen wrench.

   e) Anti-static cleaning wipes, anti-static wrist band, flashlight, and cotton swabs.

---

4. **What device has a thin needle that swings in an arc and points to a number that indicates the value of what you are measuring?**

    a) Analog multimeter

    b) Digital multimeter

    c) Loopback plug

5. **Where is the system BIOS stored?**

    a) On the primary hard drive.

    b) In CMOS RAM.

    c) On a ROM chip.

    d) In standard RAM.

6. **Which hardware components are checked during the POST?**

    a) Power supply

    b) CPU

    c) Monitor

    d) RAM

7. **True or False? Windows includes software diagnostic tests that help you find and correct hardware problems.**

    ___ True

    ___ False

Check Your Knowledge

1. When removing dust from the surface of a computer component, which cleaning tools will make it less likely for the dust to be disturbed, making it airborne?

2. Which type of multimeter, analog or digital, is better suited for measuring small variations in a computer power supply's voltage?

3. What is the relevance of the BIOS being stored in a ROM chip?

4. What types of hardware issues can result in the computer failing to POST?

_____

_____

_____

_____

EXERCISE 3-2

Identifying Electrical Safety Issues

Scenario:
In this activity, you will identify electrical safety issues.

---

1. **Which objects can help minimize ESD in a computing environment?**

   a) Air ionizer

   b) Air humidifier

   c) Insulated rubber floor mat

   d) Surge suppressor

---

2. **True or False? If you are using an anti-static floor mat, you do not need any other ESD safety equipment.**

   ___ True

   ___ False

---

3. **Electrical injuries include electrocution, shock, and collateral injury. Can you be injured if you are not part of the electrical ground current?**

---

4. **Which of these computer components present the most danger from electrical shock?**

   a) System boards

   b) Hard drives

   c) Power supplies

   d) Chassis

Check Your Knowledge

1. Why is it important to use air ionizers and humidifiers in a computing environment?

---

2. When performing computer maintenance and repairs, how can you prevent ESD from damaging the computer or one of its components?

_____

_____

_____

3. What are some of the considerations to keep in mind when using solvents and other liquids to clean computer equipment?

_____

_____

_____

_____

_____

EXERCISE 3-3

Identifying Environmental Safety Issues

Scenario:

In this activity, you will identify the best practices for promoting environmental safety and proper handling of materials.

---

1. **Match each physical hazard with the appropriate safety precaution.**

   ___ Cords and cables

   ___ Lasers

   ___ RSI

   ___ Eyestrain

   ___ Noise

   a. Avoid looking directly at them or disabling related safety equipment.

   b. Special glasses and artificial tears are viable precautionary measures.

   c. Keep printer separate from users, and use hoods.

   d. Prevent tripping by using cord protectors.

   e. Rest, therapy, surgery, and prevention are all viable solutions.

---

2. **You are on a service call, and you accidentally spill some liquid cleaner on the user's work surface. What actions should you take?**

   a) Refer to the MSDS for procedures to follow when the material is spilled.

   b) Wipe it up with a paper towel, and dispose of the paper towel in the user's trash container.

   c) Report the incident.

---

3. **Ozone is classified as an environmental hazard. What device produces ozone gas?**

   a) Laser printer

   b) CPU

   c) Laptop

   d) Power supply

---

4. **What substance reacts with heat and ammonia-based cleaners to present a workplace hazard?**

   a) Capacitors

   b) Lasers

   c) Toner

   d) Batteries

Check Your Knowledge

1. What are some of the hazards you can encounter at a job site?

   _____

   _____

   _____

2. When addressing a chemical spill, what should you do prior to cleanup and disposal of contaminated material?

   _____

   _____

3. Why are incident reports necessary?

   _____

   _____

   _____

EXERCISE 3-4

Performing Preventative Maintenance

Setup:

To complete this activity, you will need a cleaning kit consisting of:

- Monitor cleaning wipes
- Keyboard cleaning wipes
- Lint-free cloths
- Rubbing alcohol
- A mild household cleaner
- Cotton swabs (tightly wound)
- Lens cloth
- Window cleaner
- Toothpicks
- Artist's paint brush
- Compressed air canisters
- Computer vacuum
- CD-ROM cleaning kit
- Floppy drive cleaning kit

Scenario:

In an effort to cut down on the number of peripheral problems that have been occurring, your company has decided to perform preventative maintenance on peripherals each month. To help prevent other system problems, a yearly preventative maintenance plan has also been put in place to clean the internal system components, including the system board, drives, and any adapter cards. As one of the junior members of the support team, you have been assigned the task of cleaning the department's peripherals and internal system components.

 There is a simulated version of this activity available on the CD-ROM that shipped with this course. You can run this simulation on any Windows computer to review the activity after class, or as an alternative to performing the activity as a group in class. The activity simulation can be launched either directly from the CD-ROM by clicking the Interactives link and navigating to the appropriate one, or from the installed data file location by opening the C:\ 085820Data\Simulations\Lesson#\Activity# folder and double-clicking the executable (.exe) file.

What You Do	How You Do It
1. If you have a keyboard, **clean the keyboard.**	a. **Shut down the system and unplug the keyboard.**
	b. **Turn the keyboard upside down and gently shake it** to remove debris from under the keys.
	c. **Spray compressed air under the keys** to dislodge particles of dust and dirt.
	d. **Drag a small paint brush or a business card between the keys to remove any particles left behind.**
	e. **Wipe each key with keyboard wipes or a soft cloth with rubbing alcohol applied to it.**
	f. **Reconnect the keyboard and restart the system.**
	g. **Verify that all of the keys work.**

2. If you have a mouse, **clean the mouse.**

    a. **Shut down the system and unplug the mouse.**

    b. **Turn the mouse upside down and rotate the cover** to unlatch it. Rotate the cover in the direction indicated on your mouse.

    c. **Place your hand over the cover and ball, and then turn the mouse right side up and the cover and ball should drop out into your hand.** If they don't drop out, gently shake the mouse. If they still don't drop out, make sure that the cover has been turned far enough to unlatch it.

    d. Using a toothpick or your fingernail, **scrape off the line of dirt on each roller.** There should be three rollers and the dirt is usually in the center of each roller.

    e. **Spray compressed air into the mouse** to remove any remaining debris, including the debris you scraped off the rollers.

    f. **Wipe the ball, inside, outside, and the cord of the mouse with mouse cleaning wipes or a soft cloth dampened with rubbing alcohol.**

    g. **Place the ball back inside the mouse.**

    h. **Place the cover over the mouse and rotate it until it locks in place.**

    i. **Reattach the mouse and restart the system.**

    j. **Verify that all of the mouse functions work.**

3. If you have a monitor, **clean the monitor.**

> If you have an LCD monitor, do not use window cleaner on it. Instead, you should use a lint-free cloth to wipe the screen. If more cleaning power is needed, dampen the cloth with rubbing alcohol and wipe the screen.

a. **Shut down the system, turn off the monitor, and unplug the monitor cable and power cord.**

b. **Spray glass cleaner on a lint-free cloth.** Alternatively, you can use specially pre-pared wet monitor wipes and drying wipes.

c. **Wipe the monitor screen using the cloth.**

d. **Vacuum the exterior or wipe with a cloth dampened with a mild household cleaner** to remove dust and debris from the case.

e. **Reconnect the monitor to the system and plug it back in.**

f. **Restart the system and verify that the monitor works.**

4. If you have a complete PC to clean, **clean the case.**

a. **Shut down the system, and then unplug the peripherals and the power cord.**

b. **Remove the cover from the system.**

c. **Wipe the case with a water-dampened, lint-free cloth.** If the case requires addi-tional cleaning power, use a mild household cleaner on the cloth instead of water.

5. If you have a system board, **clean the system board.**

   a. **Position the system so that you can hold the compressed air canister upright.**

   b. **Spray the compressed air so that you blow the dust and debris off the system board and out of the case.**

   c. If you have a computer-safe vacuum, **vacuum any remaining particles from inside the system, being careful not to suck up any jumpers or other components.**

   d. **Reattach the case cover.**

   e. **Reconnect the external devices and power cord.**

---

6. If you have a CD-ROM drive, **clean the CD-ROM drive.**

 Refer to the instructions that come with your cleaning kit and use those steps if they are different from those listed here.

   a. **Power on the system.**

   b. **Insert the CD-ROM cleaner disk in the drive.**

   c. **Access the CD-ROM drive.**

   d. **Remove the CD-ROM cleaner disk from the drive.**

   e. **Test the drive by reading a CD-ROM.**

---

7. Clean the floppy disk drive.

   a. **Insert the floppy disk cleaner disk in the drive.**

   b. **Access the floppy disk drive.**

   c. **Remove the floppy cleaner disk from the drive.**

   d. **Test the floppy disk drive by writing to and reading from a floppy disk.**

Check Your Knowledge

1. When cleaning a CRT, what are some precautions you should follow?

   _____

   _____

   _____

   _____

2. When cleaning a standard ball mouse, where does most of the dirt typically accumulate?

   _____

   _____

   _____

3. How would you safely use compressed air when cleaning a system board?

   _____

   _____

   _____

4. What are some tools you can use to help you clean storage devices?

   _____

   _____

   _____

   _____

   _____

   _____

EXERCISE 3-5

Using a UPS

Setup:

To complete this activity, you will need a UPS.

Scenario:

There are periodic power outages at your customer's site due to old power lines and high winds. They have had several corrupted files due to power loss. They have purchased a UPS and have contracted with you to install and test it for them.

 There is a simulated version of this activity available on the CD-ROM that shipped with this course. You can run this simulation on any Windows computer to review the activity after class, or as an alternative to performing the activity as a group in class. The activity simulation can be launched either directly from the CD-ROM by clicking the Interactives link and navigating to the appropriate one, or from the installed data file location by opening the C:\085820Data\Simulations\Lesson#\Activity# folder and double-clicking the executable (.exe) file.

What You Do	How You Do It
1. **Set up the UPS to power a computer system.**	a. If necessary, **connect the battery in the UPS.**
	b. **Plug the UPS into the power outlet.**
	c. **Shut down each of the components that will be powered through the UPS.**
	d. **Unplug the components from the wall or surge protector, and then plug them into the UPS.**
	e. If your UPS is equipped with a cable to connect to a peripheral port on your computer, **connect the UPS to the USB or COM port.**

2. If the UPS comes with its own management software, **install the software.**

    a. **Insert the UPS software installation CD-ROM.**

    b. To install the software, **follow the prompts in the installation wizard.**

---

3. **Configure what happens when the UPS encounters a power failure.**

 Depending on your UPS, you might find that you must configure it using its software rather than the Power Options within Control Panel. If this is the case, complete the tasks in steps f and g within your UPS's management software.

    a. From the Start menu, **choose Control Panel.**

    b. **Click Performance And Maintenance.**

    c. **Click Power Options.**

    d. If available, **click the UPS tab.**

       If no UPS tab is displayed, **click the tab related to UPS configuration.**

    e. If necessary, **configure the UPS port, manufacturer, and model.**

    f. Following the directions that came with your UPS, or using the UPS tab in the Power Options Properties dialog box, **configure the computer to sound an alarm as soon as there is a power failure and to repeat it every minute.**

    g. **Configure the settings to perform a shutdown when the critical alarm threshold is reached.**

    h. **Close all open windows.**

---

4. **Test the UPS.**

    a. **Turn on the other components** to make sure they can be powered through the UPS.

    b. When all of the components plugged into the UPS have come up to the functional state, to simulate a power outage, **unplug the UPS from the power outlet.**

    c. **Plug the UPS back into the wall outlet.**

    d. If your UPS is equipped with a Test button, **press the Test button.**

Check Your Knowledge

1. Why would you want to plug in a USB or serial cable from the UPS to the computer?

_____

_____

_____

2. Once installed, how can you verify that the UPS is functioning properly?

_____

_____

3. What is the basic purpose of a UPS?

_____

_____

EXERCISE 3-6

Identifying Troubleshooting Best Practices

Scenario:
In this activity, you will identify general diagnostics and troubleshooting best practices that PC technicians should employ.

---

1. **When you receive notice that a user is having trouble with his computer, which is the best first step?**

   a) Determine how many users are having similar troubles.

   b) Isolate the cause of the problem.

   c) Ask the user leading questions to gather information.

   d) Check for simple solutions.

---

2. **When is a problem considered to be solved?**

   a) When the device is working correctly.

   b) When the problem has been documented.

   c) When the user is satisfied that the problem is solved.

   d) When standards are developed to prevent future occurrences of the problem.

---

3. **When troubleshooting a device problem on a Windows-based computer, what common troubleshooting tips are helpful to try first?**

Check Your Knowledge

1. Before attempting to troubleshoot any reported computer problem, what should be your first step?

---

2.   What are some things to take into account when troubleshooting?

_____

_____

_____

_____

EXERCISE 3-7

Identifying Communication and Professionalism Best Practices

Scenario:

In this activity, you will identify communication and professionalism best practices.

---

1. **Match each communication skill or behavior with the appropriate example.**

   ___ Verbal communication

   ___ Non-verbal communication

   ___ Listening skills

   ___ Respect

   ___ Ethical behavior

   ___ Confidentiality

   ___ Appearance

   a. Allow the user to complete statements without interruption.

   b. Project professionalism by being neat and clean.

   c. Do not use information gained during a service call for your personal benefit.

   d. Keep sensitive client information to yourself.

   e. Ask permission before sitting down in a user's chair or touching a user's computer.

   f. Use clear, concise, and direct statements.

   g. Maintain the proper amount of eye contact.

---

2. **Using clarifying questions to gather more information from a user is an example of what type of technique?**

   a) Passive listening

   b) Non-verbal communication

   c) Active listening

---

3. **Which are examples of displaying respect during a service call?**

   a) Asking permission before changing display settings.

   b) Asking "What happened just before you noticed the problem?"

   c) Sitting in a user's chair without permission.

   d) Turning off your pager or cell phone.

Check Your Knowledge

1. When communicating with customers, what can you do to improve communication?

   _____

   _____

2. Why is professionalism important when dealing with clients and colleagues?

   _____

   _____

3. Why is confidentiality important in this field?

   _____

   _____

   _____

   _____

   _____

LAB 3-1

Identifying PC Technician Professional Best Practices

Activity Time: 15 minutes

Scenario:

---

1. **Identify the tools in the toolkit.**

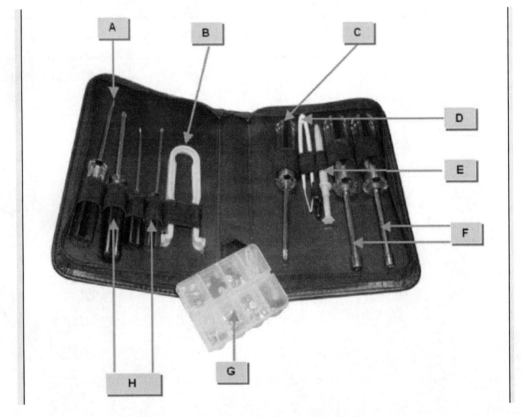

___	A	a.	Three-prong retreiver
___	B	b.	Storage container
___	C	c.	Chip extractor
___	D	d.	Nut driver
___	E	e.	Tweezers
___	F	f.	Flat head screwdriver
___	G	g.	Phillips screwdriveer
___	H	h.	Torx driver

2. **Match each computer component with the potential hazard or hazards it poses.**

___ Chassis	a.	Electrical—sharp edges can cut through insulation on wires and cables--and physical--sharp edges can cut skin.
___ Power supply	b.	Electrical—stored charges might not dissipate for long periods of time--and chemical--contains caustic electrolytes.
___ Battery	c.	Electrical—retains high voltage even when power is off if the system unit is still plugged into an electrical outlet.
___ Capacitor	d.	Electrical—remains an electrocution hazard even after the system unit is unplugged.
___ Monitor	e.	Chemical—metals used in manufacturing can cause environmental damage if improperly discarded.
___ Printer	f.	Chemical—toner can burn or melt when heated and is reactive with ammonia-based cleaners—and physical—emissions from an embedded laser can burn eyes, skin, and other objects.
___ DVD drive	g.	Physical—emissions from an embedded laser can burn eyes, skin, and other objects.

3. **Consider this scenario: A novice technician arrives at a user's workspace to trouble-shoot a sound card. The user assures the technician that the power to the PC is off. As the technician begins working, he finds that the anti-static wrist strap gets in the way, so he removes it. Once the PC cover is off, the technician pulls the sound card out of the expansion slot and places it on a nearby metal filing cabinet, replacing it with a network card that he knows works properly. Finding that the network card does not work when installed in that expansion slot, the technician determines that there is a resource conflict, corrects the conflict, and replaces the network card with the user's original sound card. After testing the sound card, the technician and user agree that the problem is resolved. As the user helps the technician clean up by spraying window cleaner on the monitor screen, she mentions a funny ozone smell coming from her laser printer. The technician assures the user that an occasional whiff of ozone is normal, and ends the service call. What would you do differently?**

4. **Which tasks are considered basic preventative maintenance tasks?**

    a) Performing inspections

    b) Updating drivers

    c) Cleaning on a scheduled basis

    d) Documenting the problem and the solution

    e) Maintaining the environment

5. **Place the troubleshooting procedures in the proper order.**

Evaluate results, and take additional steps if needed.

Analyze the problem, and make an initial determination as to the cause of the problem.

Identify the problem.

Document activities and outcomes, and verify that the user agrees that the problem is solved.

Implement the identified solution.

Test related components to solve the problem or identify a likely solution.

6. **What are some examples of active listening techniques?**

    a) Nodding your head, and maintaining eye contact

    b) Empathizing with the user

    c) Paraphrasing the user's comments

    d) Avoid interrupting the user by writing down your questions

    e) Using open-ended questions to gather information about the problem that the user is experiencing

4 | Installing and Configuring Peripheral Components

Activities included in this chapter:

- Exercise 4-1 Installing Display Devices
- Exercise 4-2 Configuring Display Devices
- Exercise 4-3 Installing Input Devices
- Exercise 4-4 Configuring Input Devices
- Exercise 4-5 Identifying System Parameters
- Exercise 4-6 Installing Adapter Cards
- Exercise 4-7 Examining Adapter Cards
- Exercise 4-8 Installing Multimedia Devices
- Exercise 4-9 Examining Multimedia Devices
- Lab 4-1 Installing and Configuring Peripheral Components

EXERCISE 4-1

Installing Display Devices

Setup:

You have a working computer with either a 15-pin VGA-style monitor port and a computer equipped with a digital video interface, or you have a digital flat-panel LCD monitor that uses the 29-pin DVI connector. The computer is turned off and the monitor is unplugged.

Scenario:

The marketing department of your company is moving to new offices, and you've been assigned the task of setting up the computers in their new offices. The computers and standard VGA CRT monitors or LCD monitors with 29-pin DVI connector have been delivered to each office. Employees want to begin using their computers as soon as possible.

 There is a simulated version of this activity available on the CD-ROM that shipped with this course. You can run this simulation on any Windows computer to review the activity after class, or as an alternative to performing the activity as a group in class. The activity simulation can be launched either directly from the CD-ROM by clicking the Interactives link and navigating to the appropriate one, or from the installed data file location by opening the C:\085820Data\Simulations\Lesson#\Activity# folder and double-clicking the executable (.exe) file.

What You Do	How You Do It
1. Install the monitor.	a. **Verify that the power is off at the computer.**
	b. **Locate the monitor cable and examine the connector.**
	c. If you have a standard VGA CRT monitor, **locate the VGA adapter port on the computer.** If you have an LCD monitor with 29-pin DVI connector, **locate the DVI port on the computer.**
	d. **Insert the monitor connector into the appropriate port, being sure to align the pins carefully.**

 It's easy to bend the pins, so align them carefully. Bent pins can result in poor video display or no video display at all.

	e. **Tighten the screws.**
	f. **Plug in the monitor.**
2. Verify that the monitor is functional.	a. **Turn on the computer power.**
	b. **Turn on the monitor power.**
	c. After the system has started to boot, **verify that the power light on the monitor is green and is not flashing.**
	d. **Watch the monitor and verify that the display is clear.**

Check Your Knowledge

1. How can you identify whether you have a standard VGA port or a DVI port?

_____

_____

_____

2. Why do you need to be careful when connecting and disconnecting display devices from the video adapter port in the back of a computer?

_____

_____

3. What does a blinking LED on a display monitor usually signify?

_____

_____

EXERCISE 4-2

Configuring Display Devices

Setup:

Your instructor has altered the display settings for your monitor. The computer is running, and the Welcome screen is displayed.

Scenario:

A monitor was recently moved from the old location to the new location. The employee reports that the display does not appear in the center of the monitor. The images are too dark, making it difficult to see, and he can't see as much on the screen as he would like. The icons on the screen are too small and the font is too big. The employee needs you to resolve these issues so that he can get back to work.

 There is a simulated version of this activity available on the CD-ROM that shipped with this course. You can run this simulation on any Windows computer to review the activity after class, or as an alternative to performing the activity as a group in class. The activity simulation can be launched either directly from the CD-ROM by clicking the Interactives link and navigating to the appropriate one, or from the installed data file location by opening the C:\085820Data\Simulations\Lesson#\Activity# folder and double-clicking the executable (.exe) file.

What You Do	How You Do It
1. **Adjust the monitor display.**	a. **Log on as Admin##.**
	b. Referring to documentation as necessary, **locate the control to adjust the brightness of the display image.**
	c. **Adjust the brightness so that the monitor is comfortable to view.**
	d. **Adjust the contrast so that you can view all screen elements easily.**

2. **Adjust the horizontal and vertical position of the image.**

   a. Referring to documentation as necessary, **locate the controls to adjust the size and centering of the display image.**

   b. **Adjust the vertical display position so that the display is centered top-to-bottom on the screen.**

   c. **Adjust the horizontal display position so that the display is centered side-to-side on the screen.**

   d. **Adjust the height and width of the image so that there is either no border or the smallest border allowed.**

3. **Change the resolution.**

   a. To open the Display Properties Control Panel, **right-click the Desktop, and choose Properties.**

   b. **Click the Settings tab.**

   c. In the Screen Resolution box, **drag the slider to the left or click to select a screen area that is less than the one currently set.**

   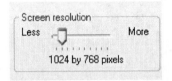

   d. **Click Apply.**

   e. If prompted, **click OK to acknowledge the informational message.**

   f. In the Monitor Settings prompt box, **click Yes.**

4. Reduce the font size.	a. Click the Appearance tab.
	b. Display the Font Size drop-down list.
	c. Select Normal.
	d. Click OK.

Check Your Knowledge

1. Where in Windows do you change a monitor's display resolution?

_____

_____

_____

2. If a user with a visual disability needs a larger font size, how can you adjust the display so that the change is reflected globally in all Windows functions and programs?

_____

_____

3. How can you adjust a display's horizontal and vertical position in Windows?

_____

_____

EXERCISE 4-3

Installing Input Devices

Setup:

For this activity, you will need a replacement keyboard and mouse or other pointing device.

Scenario:

You have received a service call to replace a user's mouse and keyboard.

 There is a simulated version of this activity available on the CD-ROM that shipped with this course. You can run this simulation on any Windows computer to review the activity after class, or as an alternative to performing the activity as a group in class. The activity simulation can be launched either directly from the CD-ROM by clicking the Interactives link and navigating to the appropriate one, or from the installed data file location by opening the C:\ 085820Data\Simulations\Lesson#\Activity# folder and double-clicking the executable (.exe) file.

What You Do	How You Do It
1. Replace the keyboard.	a. Shut down the computer, and remove the power cord.
	b. Determine the connection type used by the replacement keyboard.
	c. Unplug the old keyboard from the system unit.
	d. Plug the new keyboard into the appropriate PS/2 or USB port.
2. Replace the mouse or pointing device.	a. Determine the connection type used by the replacement mouse.
	b. Unplug the old mouse from the system unit.
	c. Plug the new mouse into the appropriate PS/2 or USB port.

Check Your Knowledge

1. What considerations should you take into account prior to replacing a mouse or keyboard?

   _____

   _____

2. After installing a new mouse or keyboard, what should you do prior to concluding the job?

   _____

   _____

   _____

   _____

   _____

EXERCISE 4-4

Configuring Input Devices

Scenario:
You just replaced a user's mouse and keyboard. The user is left-handed and prefers a slow-blinking cursor. She also has a hard time distinguishing the mouse pointer from other screen elements, and asks if you can adjust the pointers to something more easily discernible.

 There is a simulated version of this activity available on the CD-ROM that shipped with this course. You can run this simulation on any Windows computer to review the activity after class, or as an alternative to performing the activity as a group in class. The activity simulation can be launched either directly from the CD-ROM by clicking the Interactives link and navigating to the appropriate one, or from the installed data file location by opening the C:\085820Data\Simulations\Lesson#\Activity# folder and double-clicking the executable (.exe) file.

What You Do	How You Do It
1. **Configure the keyboard setting.**	a. **Choose Start→Control Panel. Click Printers and Other Hardware, and then click Keyboard.**
	b. On the Speed tab, **drag the Cursor Blink Rate slider to the third tick mark from the left.**

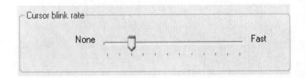

c. **Click OK.**

2. Configure the mouse settings.

a. In the Printers And Other Hardware Control Panel, **click Mouse.**

b. On the Buttons tab, **check Switch Primary And Secondary Buttons.**

c. **Right-click the Pointers tab.**

d. In the Scheme drop-down list, **select Magnified (System Scheme).**

e. **Click OK.**

f. **Readjust the mouse settings to suit your personal preferences.**

g. **Close the Control Panel window.**

Check Your Knowledge

1. A user is complaining that his mouse moves too fast, making it difficult to navigate software. How can you correct the situation?

   _____

2. You have been asked to adjust a user's keyboard to increase the repeat rate. How can you adjust this keyboard option?

   _____

   _____

EXERCISE 4-5

Identifying System Parameters

Scenario:

In preparation for adding a new device to your system, you want to check the current communication parameter assignments.

 There is a simulated version of this activity available on the CD-ROM that shipped with this course. You can run this simulation on any Windows computer to review the activity after class, or as an alternative to performing the activity as a group in class. The activity simulation can be launched either directly from the CD-ROM by clicking the Interactives link and navigating to the appropriate one, or from the installed data file location by opening the C:\085820Data\Simulations\Lesson#\Activity# folder and double-clicking the executable (.exe) file.

What You Do	How You Do It
1. **Open Device Manager.**	a. **Choose Start→Control Panel.**
	b. **Click Performance And Maintenance.**
	c. **Click System.**
	d. **Click the Hardware tab.**
	e. **Click Device Manager.**
2. **View the current DMA, IRQ, I/O address, and base memory assignments.**	a. **Choose View→Resources By Type.**
	b. To examine the current DMA assignments on your computer, **expand Direct Memory Access (DMA).**

Direct memory access (DMA)
　　2　Standard floppy disk controller
　　4　Direct memory access controller

c. To examine the current I/O address assignments on your computer, **expand Input/Output (IO).**

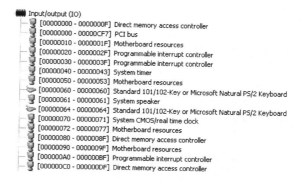

d. **Collapse Input/Output (IO).**

e. To examine the current IRQ assignments on your computer, **collapse Direct Memory Access (DMA), and expand Interrupt Request (IRQ).**

f. **Collapse Interrupt Request (IRQ).**

g. To examine the current base memory assignments on your computer, **expand Memory.**

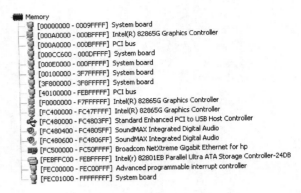

3. **Close Device Manager, System Properties, and Control Panel.**

   a. **Close Device Manager.**

   b. **Click Cancel.**

   c. **Close Control Panel.**

Check Your Knowledge

1. Why would you want to view resource usage in Device Manager?

_____

_____

2. What kind of information is displayed on the Device Manager screen?

_____

_____

EXERCISE 4-6

Installing Adapter Cards

Setup:

You have open ISA, PCI, and AGP slots on the system board. You have been given one or more of the following card types and device drivers: ISA, PCI, or AGP card.

Scenario:

You have been asked to install several expansion cards in a user's system. The appropriate drivers for the card are also available to you should you need them.

 There is a simulated version of this activity available on the CD-ROM that shipped with this course. You can run this simulation on any Windows computer to review the activity after class, or as an alternative to performing the activity as a group in class. The activity simulation can be launched either directly from the CD-ROM by clicking the Interactives link and navigating to the appropriate one, or from the installed data file location by opening the C:\ 085820Data\Simulations\Lesson#\Activity# folder and double-clicking the executable (.exe) file.

What You Do	How You Do It
1. Open the system cover and access the slots.	a. Turn off the system power.
	b. Unplug the computer from the electrical outlet.
	c. Unplug peripherals from the system.
	d. Remove the cover.
	e. Determine if you need to move or remove any components in order to access the slots.

2. **Insert the card in an available slot.**

 Do not rock the card side-to-side when installing or removing it.

a. **Locate an open slot.**

b. **Remove the slot cover.**

c. **Firmly press the card into the slot.**

d. **Secure the card to the chassis with the screw from the slot cover.** Normally, you would now secure the cover back on to the system, but since you will be doing more work inside the system, leave it off.

3. **Configure the card for the computer.**

a. **Reconnect the peripherals and cables you disconnected in step 1.**

b. **Power on the system.**

c. **Install any required drivers.**

d. **Configure DMA, I/O addresses, and/or interrupts as required for the device.**

4. **Verify that the card is functioning properly.**

a. **Connect any devices to the card that are required for testing the card functionality.**

b. **Access or use the device connected to the card.**

c. In Device Manager, **verify that the device's properties show that the device is working properly and that there are no IRQ, I/O address, or DMA conflicts, and then click Cancel.**

Check Your Knowledge

1. When installing an adapter card, what should be the first step you take?

_____

_____

2. What steps should you take once the card is firmly seated in the slot and before powering up?

_____

_____

_____

EXERCISE 4-7

Examining Adapter Cards

Scenario:
In this activity, you will examine adapter cards.

1. **Which of the following adapter cards provide interfaces necessary to connect SCSI, serial, USB, and parallel devices for data input and output?**

   a) Input/output adapters

   b) Multimedia adapters

   c) Video adapters

   d) Modem adapters

2. **True or False? Before attempting to install an adapter card, verify that the computer has an available slot that matches the adapter card's bus type.**

   ___ True

   ___ False

3. **What is the first step when installing an adapter card?**

   a) Refer to the system documentation for the procedure for the specific adapter card.

   b) Remove the system cover and access the slots on the system board.

   c) Remove the slot cover from an empty slot.

   d) Determine the unused IRQ, DMA, and I/O addresses that can be assigned to the card if needed.

Check Your Knowledge

1. What is the purpose of I/O adapter cards?

   _____

   _____

2. What considerations must you take into account before attempting to add an adapter to a computer?

   _____

   _____

   _____

EXERCISE 4-8

Installing Multimedia Devices

Setup:

If your computer does not have integrated (onboard) sound support, a sound card has been installed in your computer.

Scenario:

A group in the marketing department is responsible for creating and presenting audio visual presentations. These users have sound cards installed in their systems. They all have speakers and microphones connected to their sound cards. Some of them also have MIDI instruments and instruments that connect through an eighth-inch stereo jack. The users have just received these sound devices and want to begin using them.

 There is a simulated version of this activity available on the CD-ROM that shipped with this course. You can run this simulation on any Windows computer to review the activity after class, or as an alternative to performing the activity as a group in class. The activity simulation can be launched either directly from the CD-ROM by clicking the Interactives link and navigating to the appropriate one, or from the installed data file location by opening the C:\ 085820Data\Simulations\Lesson#\Activity# folder and double-clicking the executable (.exe) file.

What You Do	How You Do It
1. Connect the speakers to the computer.	a. Determine if you need to connect the speakers to each other, and if so, connect them to each other.
	b. Locate the speaker jack on the computer.
	c. Plug the speaker cable into the jack.
2. Connect a microphone to the MIC jack.	a. Locate the MIC jack on the computer.
	b. Connect the microphone to the MIC jack.

3.	If you have a MIDI device, **connect the MIDI device through the game port.**	a. **Locate the game port.**
		b. **Connect the MIDI adapter to the game port.**
		c. If necessary, **connect MIDI cables to the MIDI adapter.**
		d. **Connect the MIDI cable to the MIDI instrument.**
		e. If necessary, **install drivers for the MIDI instrument.**
4.	**Connect an external device to the Line In jack.**	a. **Locate the Line In jack.**
		b. **Connect an eighth-inch stereo jack from the device to the computer.**
5.	**Test the sound components.**	a. To test the microphone, **choose Start→ All Programs→ Accessories→ Entertainment→Sound Recorder.**
		b. In the Sound Recorder window, **click the Record button.**
		c. **Speak a few words into the microphone.**
		d. **Click the Stop button.**
		e. To test the speakers, **click the Play button.** The words you just recorded should be played back.
		f. If you installed a MIDI device, **play a few notes to verify that it works correctly.**
		g. **Close the Sound Recorder without saving changes.**

Check Your Knowledge

1. When installing external audio devices on a computer, how can you identify what each audio port is for?

   _____

   _____

2. When installing or configuring audio devices, how can you test audio functionality?

   _____

   _____

   _____

EXERCISE 4-9

Examining Multimedia Devices

Scenario:
In this activity, you will examine multimedia devices.

1. **When installing multimedia devices, how do you connect an external device to the system?**

    a) Connect it to the line jack.

    b) Connect it to the MIC jack.

    c) Connect it through the game port.

    d) Connect it to the jack on the sound card.

2. **True or False? When installing a sound card, you don't have to worry about the available slots on the motherboard.**

    __ True

    __ False

Check Your Knowledge

1. What is the difference between a MIC and a Line In jack?

    _____

    _____

    _____

    _____

2. When helping a user to select a speaker system, what are some things to consider?

    _____

    _____

    _____

LAB 4-1

Installing and Configuring Peripheral Components

Activity Time: 1 hour(s), 15 minutes

Objective:
Install and configure computer components.

Scenario:

 You can find a suggested solution for this activity in the \Solutions\Installing and Configuring Peripheral Components.txt file in the data file location.

1. **Install and configure a monitor.**

2. **Install and configure the keyboard and mouse.**

3. **Install and configure a multimedia device.**

5 | Installing and Configuring System Components

Activities included in this chapter:

- Exercise 5-1 Selecting a Storage Device
- Exercise 5-2 Installing Internal Storage Devices
- Exercise 5-3 Replacing a Power Supply
- Exercise 5-4 Examining Power Supplies
- Exercise 5-5 Determining the Appropriate Type of RAM
- Exercise 5-6 Adding RAM to a Computer
- Exercise 5-7 Examining Memory
- Exercise 5-8 Upgrading the CPU
- Exercise 5-9 Examining CPUs
- Exercise 5-10 Upgrading the System Board
- Exercise 5-11 Examining System Boards
- Lab 5-1 Installing and Configuring System Components

EXERCISE 5-1

Selecting a Storage Device

Scenario:
You're servicing a customer's computers. You have been asked to order storage devices to upgrade a number of the computers.

1. **You have been asked to order an internal hard drive for one of the customer's computers. The customer has heard about the increased performance of SATA drives and would like you to purchase one for the computer. What question should you ask first before ordering a new SATA hard drive?**

   a) Does the computer have an available drive bay for the drive?

   b) Does the computer have an available power supply cable for the new drive?

   c) Does the computer have existing storage devices?

   d) Do you have the necessary data cable to connect the drive to the controller?

2. **True or False? You can attach a Serial ATA hard drive as a second drive on a Parallel ATA data cable.**

   ___ True

   ___ False

3. **A user wants to transfer several megabytes of data between two computers that are not connected by a network. What storage device would you recommend?**

   a) A USB thumb drive.

   b) A floppy disk.

   c) An external tape drive.

   d) An internal optical drive.

Check Your Knowledge

1. What steps should you take before upgrading a customer's hard drive?

   _____

   _____

   _____

2. Which devices can you use to replace the floppy disk drive's portability and flexibility?

_____

_____

EXERCISE 5-2

Installing Internal Storage Devices

Setup:

To complete this activity, you will need the following hardware components. If you do not have these available, you can remove and reinstall the existing hardware.

- A second hard drive and an empty drive bay. If you have a Parallel ATA drive, you will also need an available connection on the Parallel ATA cable. If you have a SCSI drive, you will also need an installed SCSI host bus adapter (HBA).

- A floppy disk drive that is compatible with your system.

- An optical drive that is compatible with your system.

- Available power connections for the devices you are adding to the system.

- Optionally, rails to allow smaller drives to fit into larger drive bays.

Scenario:

You have been assigned the task of refurbishing a computer for a user. This computer has a single functioning hard drive, a floppy disk drive that needs to be replaced, and an optical drive that needs to be replaced. The user needs a significant amount of local storage space, and the following internal storage devices have been allocated for use in this project:

- A second hard disk drive

- A floppy drive

- A Parallel ATA optical drive

 There is a simulated version of this activity available on the CD-ROM that shipped with this course. You can run this simulation on any Windows computer to review the activity after class, or as an alternative to performing the activity as a group in class. The activity simulation can be launched either directly from the CD-ROM by clicking the Interactives link and navigating to the appropriate one, or from the installed data file location by opening the C:\085820Data\Simulations\Lesson#\Activity# folder and double-clicking the executable (.exe) file.

What You Do	How You Do It

Add a hard disk drive to the system

1. **Locate available bay, power, and data connection resources for the new hard disk drive.**

   a. **Power off the system, unplug all peripherals and the power cord, and open the computer case.**

   b. **Locate an available drive bay and determine if the bay is the same form factor as the drive.** If you are using a 5.25-inch drive bay and a 3.5-inch drive, you will need to install the drive using rails to adapt the drive to the larger bay.

   c. **Locate an available data connection on the data cable.** If necessary, **connect a Parallel ATA data cable to the Parallel ATA controller connection on the system board.**

   d. **Locate an available power connector.** If necessary, **connect a power splitter to an existing power connection.**

2. **Prepare the drive for installation.**

   a. If you are installing a Parallel ATA drive, **set the jumpers or switches to Cable Select or Slave.**

   b. If you are installing a SCSI drive, **set the SCSI ID to an unused ID number.** If the drive is at the end of the SCSI chain, **terminate the device** and, if necessary, **remove termination from the previously terminated device.**

   c. If necessary, **attach rails to the drive to fit in the bay.**

3. **Install the hard disk drive into the system.**

   a. **Slide the drive into the bay.**

   b. **Connect the data cable to the drive.**

   c. **Connect the power cable to the drive.**

   d. **Secure the drive to the bay chassis with screws.**

4. **Verify that the drive is accessible.**

a. **Plug all peripherals back into the system.**

 You can leave the case open until the end of the activity.

b. **Restart the system.**

c. If prompted, **access CMOS, set the disk type according to the drive documentation, and then exit CMOS and save your settings.**

5. **Partition and format the new drive as an NTFS drive.**

a. **Log on to Windows as Admin##.**

b. **On the Desktop, right-click My Computer and choose Manage.**

c. In the left pane, **click Disk Management.**

d. **Right-click the unallocated space for Disk 1.** The new disk is all unallocated.

e. **Choose New Partition.** The New Partition Wizard starts.

f. **Click Next.**

g. **With Primary Partition selected, click Next.**

h. **Accept the defaults for partition size and click Next.**

i. **Accept the default drive letter and click Next.**

j. **Format the partition as NTFS using Default as the Allocation Unit Size and New Volume as the Volume Label. Click Next.**

k. **Click Finish.**

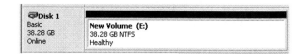

l. **Close Disk Management.**

Replace the floppy disk drive

6. **Remove the floppy disk drive from the computer.**	a. **Shut down the computer, and unplug the power cord from the power supply.**
	b. **Disconnect the power connector from the rear of the floppy disk drive.**
	c. **Disconnect the controller cable from the rear of the floppy disk drive.**
	d. **Remove the screws, brackets, or clips that mount the floppy disk drive in the chassis bay.**
	e. If necessary, **remove the front cover.**
	f. **Slide the disk drive out of its bay.**
	g. **Examine the controller cable connectors and power cable connector on the rear of the drive.** This data cable and power cable are different than those used on the hard drives.
7. **Connect the new floppy drive to the system.**	a. **Insert the floppy disk drive into its bay.**
	b. **Mount the floppy disk drive to the chassis using the appropriate screws, brackets, or clips.**
	c. **Connect the controller cable to the rear of the floppy disk drive.**
	d. **Connect the power connector to the rear of the floppy disk drive.**
	e. **Reconnect the power cord to the power supply, start the system, and verify that the floppy disk drive was properly installed.**

 To verify the floppy disk drive is functional, you can try to access data from a floppy disk or open My Computer to verify that the A drive is visible.

Replace the optical drive

8. Remove the old optical drive from the computer.	a. Shut down the computer, and unplug the power cord from the power supply.
	b. Disconnect the power connector from the rear of the optical drive.
	c. Disconnect the controller cable from the rear of the optical drive.
	d. Disconnect the audio cable from the rear of the optical drive.
	e. Remove the screws, brackets, or clips that mount the optical drive in the chassis bay.
	f. Slide the optical drive out of its bay.

9. **Install the new optical drive in the computer.**

   a. If you are installing a Parallel ATA optical drive, **examine the controller cable connectors and the jumper block for master/slave configuration on the rear of the drive. Verify that the optical drive is set as master/single.**

   b. If you are installing a SCSI optical drive, **set the SCSI ID to an unused ID number. If the drive is at the end of the SCSI chain, terminate the device** and, if necessary, **remove termination from the previously terminated device.**

   c. **Insert the optical drive into its bay.**

   d. **Mount the optical drive to the chassis using the appropriate screws, brackets, or clips.**

   e. **Connect the controller cable to the rear of the optical drive. Make sure the colored stripe on the controller cable lines up with Pin 1 on the drive.**

   f. **Connect the audio cable to the audio out connector at the rear of the optical drive.**

   g. **Connect the power connector to the rear of the optical drive.**

      Reconnect the power cord to the power supply, and start the system.

   h. **Verify that you can read data from the optical drive.**

   i. **Close the computer case.**

Check Your Knowledge

1. Before installing a new hard drive into a system with an existing hard drive, what physical considerations must you take into account?

    _____

    _____

    _____

    _____

2. After installing an additional hard drive, what steps must you take in order to make it usable?

_____

3. How do you replace removable drives such as CD-ROM drives or floppy disk drives?

_____
_____
_____
_____
_____

EXERCISE 5-3

Replacing a Power Supply

Setup:

You have a power supply to install into the system. If you don't have another power supply, you can just reinstall the one you take out.

Scenario:

After calculating the power needed for all of the components added to a user's system, you have determined that it exceeds the capacity of the installed power supply.

 There is a simulated version of this activity available on the CD-ROM that shipped with this course. You can run this simulation on any Windows computer to review the activity after class, or as an alternative to performing the activity as a group in class. The activity simulation can be launched either directly from the CD-ROM by clicking the Interactives link and navigating to the appropriate one, or from the installed data file location by opening the C:\085820Data\Simulations\Lesson#\Activity# folder and double-clicking the executable (.exe) file.

What You Do	How You Do It
1. **Remove the existing power supply.**	a. **Shut down and turn off the system.**
	b. **Unplug the power cord from the electrical outlet.**
	c. To discharge any remaining electricity stored in the computer's capacitors, **toggle the power switch on the computer on and off.**
	d. **Remove any components necessary in order to access the power supply and its connection to the system board.**
	e. **Unplug all power connections from devices, marking where each connection went to as you go.**
	f. **Unplug the power supply from the system board.**
	g. **Unscrew the power supply from the case.**
	h. **Remove the power supply from the case.**
2. **Install the replacement power supply.**	a. **Insert the power supply into the case.**
	b. **Secure the power supply to the case.**
	c. **Plug all power connections into the devices.**
	d. **Plug the power supply into the system board.**
	e. **Reinstall any components you removed to access the power supply.**
	f. **Plug the power cord from the power supply to the electrical outlet.**

3. **Test the power supply.**	**a.** **Turn on the system.**
	b. **Log on as Administrator.**
	c. **Test all components.**

Check Your Knowledge

1. Prior to replacing a power supply, it is necessary to drain all power from the computer. How do you discharge all remaining power that might be stored in the capacitors, even after unplugging the computer?

   _____

   _____

   _____

2. Is replacing a power supply a complicated task requiring removal of most of the computer's internal components?

   _____

   _____

   _____

EXERCISE 5-4

Examining Power Supplies

Scenario:
In this activity, you will examine power supplies.

1. **When determining the amount of power needed for a computer system, which components should you include?**

   a) CPU

   b) RAM

   c) System board

   d) Expansion cards

   e) Peripheral devices

2. **When installing and configuring a power supply, what step should you complete first?**

   a) Unplug the power supply from the system board.

   b) Unplug the electrical power cord from the electric outlet and from the power supply.

   c) Toggle the power switch on the computer on and off to discharge any remaining electricity stored in the computer's capacitors.

   d) Shut down and turn off the system.

Check Your Knowledge

1. How can you determine how much power is required when purchasing a new power supply?

   _____

   _____

   _____

   _____

2. After installing a new power supply, and prior to powering up the system, what precautions must you take?

   _____

   _____

   _____

EXERCISE 5-5

Determining the Appropriate Type of RAM

Scenario:
You've been asked to help another A+ technician determine the type and quantity of RAM to be ordered. He has several questions he needs you to answer before he is able to place the order with the vendor.

1. **Match the type of RAM with its description.**

   ___ VRAM

   ___ DDR SDRAM

   ___ SRAM

   ___ DRAM

   ___ SAM

   a. A replacement for SDRAM.

   b. A special type of DRAM used on video cards that can be written to and read from at the same time. It also requires less refreshing than normal DRAM.

   c. Volatile memory that holds data in a sequential order.

   d. Used for cache memory. It does not need to be refreshed to retain information. It can use synchronous, asynchronous, burst, or pipeline burst technologies.

   e. Used on SIMMs and DIMMs. It needs to be refreshed every few milliseconds. Uses assigned memory addresses.

2. **True or False? RAM will not run any faster than the system board's bus speed.**

   ___ True

   ___ False

3. **True or False? A nanosecond is one-trillionth of a second.**

   ___ True

   ___ False

4. **In a system that contains RAM modules that run at 6 ns and 10 ns, what speed will the RAM run at?**

   a) 4 ns

   b) 10 ns

   c) 6 ns

   d) 16 ns

5. **On a typical system with RAM that runs at a speed of 10 ns, you could add RAM that runs at which speed?**

   a) 6 ns

   b) 10 ns

   c) 12 ns

6. **The number of SIMMs or DIMMs needed to create a bank is the width of the CPUs data bus divided by the width of the _____ __ _____ .**

7. **On a system with a CPU with a 64-bit data bus, how many SIMMs would you need to create a bank?**

   a) 2

   b) 4

   c) 8

   d) 16

8. **On a system with a CPU with a 32-bit data bus, how many SIMMs would you need to create a bank?**

   a) 2

   b) 4

   c) 8

   d) 16

Check Your Knowledge

1. A customer wants to purchase faster RAM for his computer. How can you determine the fastest speed that the system board will support?

   _____

   _____

2. Before purchasing new RAM, what kind of information should you have available?

   _____

   _____

   _____

EXERCISE 5-6

Adding RAM to a Computer

Scenario:

The computers your organization purchased have been performing sluggishly. Additional RAM has been purchased for these computers.

 There is a simulated version of this activity available on the CD-ROM that shipped with this course. You can run this simulation on any Windows computer to review the activity after class, or as an alternative to performing the activity as a group in class. The activity simulation can be launched either directly from the CD-ROM by clicking the Interactives link and navigating to the appropriate one, or from the installed data file location by opening the C:\085820Data\Simulations\Lesson#\Activity#folder and double-clicking the executable (.exe) file.

What You Do	How You Do It
1. **Determine how much RAM is currently installed.**	a. If necessary, **log in to the computer as Admin## with a password of** *!Pass1234* (where the *##* is your student number). b. From the Start menu, **choose My Computer.** c. **Click View System Information.**

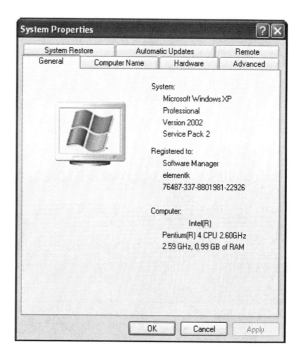

---

2. **How much memory is currently installed?**

_____

_____

_____

3.	**Install more memory in the system.**	a. **Shut down your computer.**
		b. **Disconnect the power cord.**
		c. **Discharge any static electricity from yourself and your clothes.**
		d. **Locate the memory expansion sockets in your system.**
		e. If there are no empty memory expansion sockets or you don't have a memory module to practice with, **push the ejector tabs on each end of the memory module out** to release the memory module, **and then remove the memory module.**
		f. **Align the notched edge of the memory module with the memory expansion slot, and then firmly press the module down into the socket.**
		g. If the ejector tabs did not automatically lock into each end of the memory module, **push both ejector tabs up until they lock into the notches on each end of the memory module.**
4.	**Verify that the additional memory is recognized by the system.**	a. **Plug in the power cord and restart the system.**
		b. If prompted at startup, **follow any on-screen prompts** to make the system recognize the memory.
		c. **Display the System Properties dialog box and record the amount of memory shown.** If the additional memory isn't recognized, you can check documentation to see if any steps need to be performed. Also, verify that the memory was correctly seated in the slots and was the correct type of memory for the system.

Check Your Knowledge

1. How can you verify how much RAM is currently installed on a computer without opening the chassis and examining the memory modules?

    _____

    _____

2. When installing any RAM on a system board, what precautions must you take?

    _____

    _____

    _____

EXERCISE 5-7

Examining Memory

Scenario:
In this activity, you will examine how memory is installed and configured.

---

1. **True or False? If there are no empty memory expansion sockets on the system board, you will need to remove an existing module and replace it with a module that contains more memory.**

   ___ True

   ___ False

---

2. **Where can you verify how much RAM is currently installed on your computer?**

   a) System Properties

   b) Component Services

   c) Services

   d) CMOS Settings

Check Your Knowledge

1. You have determined that you can add additional memory to a computer, but there are no empty slots left. What options do you have?

   _____

   _____

   _____

EXERCISE 5-8

Upgrading the CPU

Scenario:

One of your clients has an older computer that needs to be upgraded. The CPU in the computer doesn't meet the requirements for the application the client needs to run. The client has purchased a CPU upgrade and would like you to install it.

 There is a simulated version of this activity available on the CD-ROM that shipped with this course. You can run this simulation on any Windows computer to review the activity after class, or as an alternative to performing the activity as a group in class. The activity simulation can be launched either directly from the CD-ROM by clicking the Interactives link and navigating to the appropriate one, or from the installed data file location by opening the C:\ 085820Data\Simulations\Lesson#\Activity# folder and double-clicking the executable (.exe) file.

What You Do	How You Do It
1. Remove the existing CPU.	a. **Shut down the system and unplug the power cord.**

 If you have a slot based CPU, follow your instructor's recommendations to remove and then install the processor.

b. If necessary, **undo the clip to remove the heat sink and fan from the top of the CPU.**

c. If necessary, **unplug the power cable from the CPU fan.**

d. **Pull up the lever on the side of the ZIF-socket CPU.** If you have a different style CPU, refer to the system documentation for how to remove it.

e. Now that the CPU has been released, **pick the CPU straight up** so as not to bend any pins.

f. **Place the old CPU in a safe location in an appropriate container** to prevent damage to the CPU should you need or want to reinstall it later.

2. **Install the replacement CPU.**

    a. **On the system board, align the pins on the CPU with the holes in the ZIF socket.**

    b. **Press the CPU lever back down** to lock the CPU in place.

    c. **Lock the heat sink and fan clip.**

    d. **Plug the CPU fan power plug in to the system board.**

    e. **Connect any power connections to the appropriate power connectors.**

3. **Verify that the CPU is recognized.**

    a. **Restart the system.**

    b. **Display the System Properties dialog box.**

    c. **Verify that the CPU listed on the General page matches what you just installed.**

Check Your Knowledge

1. When installing a new CPU, what general precautions must you take to avoid damaging the CPU?

   _____

   _____

   _____

2. After installing a new CPU, what critical precaution must you take prior to powering up the system?

   _____

   _____

   _____

3. Once you power up the system, what is a clear sign that there is a problem with the CPU installation?

   _____

   _____

EXERCISE 5-9

Examining CPUs

Scenario:

In this activity, you will examine CPUs.

---

1. **When you install a new CPU in a system, what is the first thing you should do?**

   a) Shut down the system.

   b) Ground yourself to dissipate any static electricity.

   c) Unplug the power cord.

   d) Pull up the lever on the side of the ZIF-socket CPU.

---

2. **True or False? When installing a CPU, verify that you have the necessary equipment to cool the new processor.**

   ___ True

   ___ False

Check Your Knowledge

1. Prior to installing a CPU, what steps should you take?

   _____

   _____

   _____

2. What CPU cooling considerations must you take into account when installing a new CPU?

   _____

   _____

EXERCISE 5-10

Upgrading the System Board

Scenario:

A lightning storm destroyed the system board in one of your customers' systems. You have been assigned the task of replacing the system board. While doing so, the customer would like you to put in an upgraded system board to improve system performance.

 There is a simulated version of this activity available on the CD-ROM that shipped with this course. You can run this simulation on any Windows computer to review the activity after class, or as an alternative to performing the activity as a group in class. The activity simulation can be launched either directly from the CD-ROM by clicking the Interactives link and navigating to the appropriate one, or from the installed data file location by opening the C:\ 085820Data\Simulations\Lesson#\Activity# folder and double-clicking the executable (.exe) file.

 When installing new equipment, follow the instructions included with the device from the manufacturer.

What You Do	How You Do It
1. Remove cards and cables.	a. Shut down the computer and unplug the power cord.
	b. Disconnect all external devices.
	c. Open the computer case.

 You may find it helpful at this point to take a picture of the inside of the computer to use as reference later.

d. **Remove all cards from the expansion slots and store them in appropriate anti-static containers.**

e. As you disconnect each cable in the computer, **attach a piece of masking tape to each cable and record where each connection goes as you remove it.**

f. If you need the room, **unplug the power and data cable connectors for all drives in the computer. Mark which cable is connected to the primary and which to the secondary IDE connector.**

g. **Unplug connectors attached to any front-panel switches or LEDs.**

h. **Unplug the power supply and data cables from the system board.**

i. If necessary, **remove the drive bay assembly and any other components needed to access all the screws on the system board.**

---

2. **Remove the existing system board.**

a. **Unscrew the system board from the case.** Be sure to set the screws aside to use in mounting the new system board.

b. **Lift the system board,** and then if necessary, **slide it forward, and then lift it up and out of the case.**

---

3. **Install the new system board.**

 Be sure not to screw the system board in too tightly to avoid damaging the system board.

a. **Slide the new system board into the case, aligning the mounting holes.**

b. **Secure the system board to the case using the screws you removed from the old system board.**

 Start all the screws before you begin tightening them.

| 4. | Install RAM and a processor on the new system board. | a. | Install the memory modules beginning with the first memory slot (Bank 0). |
| | | b. | Install the CPU according to the manufacturer's directions. |

5.	Reinstall the cards and cables.	a.	Reconnect all internal cables and cards, including any LED or front-panel switch connections.
		b.	Reinstall adapter cards.
		c.	If you needed to remove any drive bay assemblies or other components to access the system board, **replace any of those components.**
		d.	Reconnect the power supply to the system board.
		e.	Reconnect all external devices.

| 6. | Test the computer. | a. | Plug in the power cord. |
| | | b. | **Start the computer.** If all went well, it should boot. Windows might attempt to reboot several times as it discovers new components. |

Check Your Knowledge

1. Which components must you remove when upgrading a system board?

_____

_____

2. Once the system board is replaced, do components have to be installed in a particular order?

_____

_____

_____

_____

EXERCISE 5-11

Examining System Boards

Scenario:

In this activity, you will examine system boards.

---

1. **True or False? Often when you are examining a system board, you will find that there are very few components on the board that are actually repairable.**

    __ True

    __ False

---

2. **When you are installing or upgrading a system board, what should you do as you are disconnecting the cables from the board?**

    a) Remove them completely from the case, so they are out of the way.

    b) Mark each cable as you go, so you can easily reconnect them later.

    c) Unscrew the system board from the case.

    d) Disconnect all external devices.

Check Your Knowledge

1. How many system board components are repairable by a field technician?

    _____

    _____

    _____

2. When disconnecting cables from the system board, what precautions must you take?

    _____

    _____

LAB 5-1

Installing and Configuring System Components

Activity Time: 1 hour(s)

Scenario:

 You can find a suggested solution for this activity in the \Solutions\Installing and Configuring System Components.txt file in the data file location.

---

1. **Install and configure the storage device.** If you install a hard drive, be sure to prepare it for storing files.

---

2. **Install the power supply.**

---

3. **Install the RAM.**

---

4. **Install the CPU.**

---

5. **Install the system board.**

---

6 | Maintaining and Troubleshooting Peripheral Components

Activities included in this chapter:

- Exercise 6-1 Troubleshooting Display Devices
- Exercise 6-2 Maintaining and Troubleshooting Input Devices
- Exercise 6-3 Troubleshooting Adapter Cards
- Exercise 6-4 Troubleshooting Multimedia Devices
- Lab 6-1 Maintaining and Troubleshooting Peripheral Components

EXERCISE 6-1

Troubleshooting Display Devices

Scenario:

Several users have opened trouble tickets with the support center about problems with their monitors. All of the users need their systems fixed before they can continue with their work. You need to resolve the problems. The following is a list of the trouble tickets you are responding to.

Ticket No.	Location	User Name	Issue
296001	Main building, 31H21	Robert Allen	The user's monitor is not coming on. The power light is not lighted. The user has checked that the monitor is plugged in and the monitor is connected to the system.
296002	Main building, 13B19	Althea Gavin	User's monitor is flickering and the display is distorted.
296003	Elmwood Place, cube 32	Chris Parker	The monitor power light is on, but there is no display.
296005	Main building, 62B35	Joan Paris	The monitor is making noises.

 There is a simulated version of this activity available on the CD-ROM that shipped with this course. You can run this simulation on any Windows computer to review the activity after class, or as an alternative to performing the activity as a group in class. The activity simulation can be launched either directly from the CD-ROM by clicking the Interactives link and navigating to the appropriate one, or from the installed data file location by opening the C:\085820Data\Simulations\Lesson#\Activity# folder and double-clicking the executable (.exe) file.

What You Do	How You Do It
1. **Resolve trouble ticket 296001.**	a. **Unplug the monitor from the electrical outlet and plug in a lamp or other device** to verify that the monitor is plugged into a working outlet. If the device works, **plug the monitor back into the outlet.** If the device does not work, **contact the electrician to fix the outlet and plug the monitor in to another outlet.**
	b. If the outlet is on a UPS, surge protector, or power strip, **verify that the unit is turned on.**
	c. **Verify that the connections of the power cord and monitor cable are secure on the monitor as well as on the PC and electrical outlet.**
	d. **Try to turn on the monitor again.**
	e. If the monitor still doesn't come on, **replace the monitor with a known good monitor.**
2. **Resolve trouble ticket 296002.**	a. **Verify that the monitor cable is firmly plugged in to the monitor and to the computer.**
	b. If available, **press the Degauss button.**
	c. **Check the monitor cable for any bent pins and straighten if necessary.**
	d. **Move the monitor away from florescent light, speakers, other monitors, or other electronic devices with powerful motors.**

3. **Resolve trouble ticket 296003.**

    a. **Verify that the monitor cable is connected to the monitor and to the PC.**

    b. **Adjust the contrast using the buttons on the monitor.**

    c. **Adjust the brightness using the buttons on the monitor.**

    d. If it still is not working, **swap the monitor with one that you know works** to determine if the problem is with the monitor or the video card.

4. **Resolve trouble ticket 296005.**

    a. **Determine whether noise is crackling or whining noise.**

    b. If it is a crackling noise, **clean the monitor and try to vacuum or blow dust out of monitor vents. Do not open the monitor!** If necessary, send it out for more in-depth cleaning.

    c. If it is a whining noise, try the following to fix it: **move the monitor or change the refresh rate.** If it won't stop whining, send it out for adjustment and **replace the monitor with a quieter one.**

Check Your Knowledge

1. When troubleshooting display device power problems, what is the first step you should take?

2. What is the purpose of the degaussing button or menu option in CRT displays?

3. When troubleshooting a display device that shows it is powered up but there is no image displayed on it, what should you check for first?

EXERCISE 6-2

Maintaining and Troubleshooting Input Devices

Scenario:

Several users have opened trouble tickets with the support center about problems with their keyboards and pointing devices. All of the users need their systems fixed before they can continue with their work. You need to resolve the problems and get the users back to work. The following is a list of the trouble tickets you are responding to.

Ticket No.	Location	User Name	Issue
299001	Elmwood Place, cube 24	Al Mikels	The user's keyboard is not working at all.
299002	Training center, room 1	Andy Potarnia	User's keyboard is producing the wrong characters when he types.
299003	Main building, 42B31	Toma Wright	User's mouse jumping around on the screen.
299004	Main building, 31C93	Jason Zeh	User has a cordless mouse, and the mouse pointer is not moving on the screen.
299005	Main building, 26B15	Daniel Bidlack	Root beer has been spilled on user's keyboard.

 There is a simulated version of this activity available on the CD-ROM that shipped with this course. You can run this simulation on any Windows computer to review the activity after class, or as an alternative to performing the activity as a group in class. The activity simulation can be launched either directly from the CD-ROM by clicking the Interactives link and navigating to the appropriate one, or from the installed data file location by opening the C:\085820Data\Simulations\Lesson#\Activity# folder and double-clicking the executable (.exe) file.

What You Do	How You Do It
1. If you have been assigned trouble ticket 299001, **resolve trouble ticket 299001.**	a. **Verify that the keyboard is plugged in to the keyboard port.** b. **Verify that the keyboard cable is securely connected.** c. If the keyboard still does not work, **switch with a known good keyboard.** d. If the keyboard still does not work, **verify that the keyboard is recognized by the CMOS.** e. If the keyboard still does not work, **replace the system board.**
2. If you have been assigned trouble ticket 299002, **resolve trouble ticket 299002.**	a. **Verify that no Function key, Scroll Lock, or other key is enabled or stuck down.** b. If that is not the problem, **replace keyboard with a known good keyboard.**
3. If you have been assigned trouble ticket 299003, **resolve trouble ticket 299003.**	a. **Make sure the surface the mouse is being rolled on is clean and smooth.** b. **Clean the rollers inside the mouse.** c. **Clean the mouse ball by blowing on it or by using warm water and mild detergent.** d. From the Start menu, **choose Control Panel. Click Printers And Other Hardware. Click Mouse. Check the pointer speed, click speed, and other settings that might affect performance.** e. If the problem is not resolved, **replace the mouse.**

4. If you have been assigned trouble ticket 299004, **resolve trouble ticket 299004.**

    a. **Verify that there is no obstruction between the transmitter and receiver devices.**

    b. **Press the Reset or Connect buttons on each device to try to re-establish the connection.**

    c. **Replace the batteries in the mouse.**

    d. **Press the Reset or Connect buttons on each device.**

    e. **Verify that the receiver device is connected to the port.**

    f. **Try reinstalling the latest software or driver for the cordless mouse.**

    g. If it still has not been resolved, **try a corded mouse connected to the port.**

    h. If the previous step worked, **replace the cordless mouse with either a corded or another cordless mouse.**

5. If you have been assigned trouble ticket 299005, **resolve trouble ticket 299005.**

    a. **Remind users that all drinks must be covered when used near computer equipment.**

    b. **Unplug the keyboard and turn it upside down over the wastebasket.**

    c. **Move the keyboard around to remove as much liquid as possible.**

    d. **Rinse the keyboard in running water.**

    e. **Set on end to dry for several days.**

    f. **Swap in an alternate keyboard so the user can get back to work until the original keyboard is ready.**

Check Your Knowledge

1. When troubleshooting a user's non-functional input device, what should be your first troubleshooting step?

    _____

    _____

2. When troubleshooting input devices exhibiting erratic behavior, what should you check for?

    _____

    _____

    _____

    _____

3. When troubleshooting cordless or wireless input devices, what should you check for first?

    _____

    _____

EXERCISE 6-3

Troubleshooting Adapter Cards

Scenario:

The call center has received several trouble calls that are related to internal PC adapter card problems. You need to help resolve the problems and get the users back to work. The following is a list of the current trouble tickets.

Ticket No.	Location	User Name	Issue
399001	Main building, 33J27	Aminah Sinclair	The user is still having problems with his video system. All monitor problems were reviewed and none of these resolved the problem. Therefore, it points toward a problem with the video card.
399002	Elmwood Place, cube 14	Conroy Ives	Last night a lightning storm struck. Most equipment was fine, but this user is having problems with getting on the network. All other users in the area are connecting without problems.

 There is a simulated version of this activity available on the CD-ROM that shipped with this course. You can run this simulation on any Windows computer to review the activity after class, or as an alternative to performing the activity as a group in class. The activity simulation can be launched either directly from the CD-ROM by clicking the Interactives link and navigating to the appropriate one, or from the installed data file location by opening the C:\ 085820Data\Simulations\Lesson#\Activity# folder and double-clicking the executable (.exe) file.

What You Do	How You Do It
1. If it has been assigned to you, **respond to trouble ticket 399001.**	a. **Locate the video card and make sure it is fully seated into the slot, then see if this fixed the problem.**
	b. **Determine if the video card is in a PCI, PCI-E, or AGP slot.** If it is not in an AGP slot, **try moving the card to another slot.**
	c. If you are still having problems, **remove the card and press down on all four corners of socketed chips to verify they are fully seated, then reinstall the card.**
	d. If a hardware device has been recently added to the system, **check Device Manager and verify that there is not a resource conflict between the device and the video card.**
	e. If you are still having problems, **try a known good working video card.**
2. If it has been assigned to you, **respond to trouble ticket 399002.**	a. **Check whether the network card is listed in Device Manager.**
	b. **Display properties for the network card and verify whether the Device Status indicates it is working properly.**
	c. If the device is not working properly, **click Troubleshoot and follow the Troubleshoot Wizard steps.**
	d. If the problem is not resolved, **replace the network card.**
	e. **Verify that the system can now connect to the network.**

Check Your Knowledge

1. When performing in-depth troubleshooting of an adapter card, what steps can you take beyond verifying drivers and connectivity?

   _____

   _____

   _____

   _____

   _____

2. After installing a new adapter in an open slot, you notice there is a red X in Windows XP Professional's Device Manager. What is one common problem you do not suspect in this situation?

   _____

   _____

3. You are troubleshooting an intermittent device connected to an adapter card. What are some of the troubleshooting steps you can take?

   _____

   _____

   _____

EXERCISE 6-4

Troubleshooting Multimedia Devices

Scenario:

Two users have opened trouble tickets with the support center about problems with their speakers. You have been asked to resolve these problems. The following is a list of the trouble tickets.

Ticket No.	Location	User Name	Issue
325145	Main building, 31H21	Reilly Smith	No sound is coming out of the user's speakers. The power light on the speakers is not lit.
325146	Main building, 13B19	Alice Griffin	No sound is coming out of the user's speakers. The power light on the speakers is lit.

What You Do	How You Do It
1. If it has been assigned to you, **respond to trouble ticket 325145.**	a. **Make sure that the speakers are plugged into a power source.**
	b. **Verify that the power source is working properly by plugging a known good device into the power source.**
	c. **Try the speakers on a known good sound card.** If the speakers don't work, **replace the failed speakers on the computer.**

2. If it has been assigned to you, **respond to trouble ticket 325146.**

a. **Verify that the volume on the speakers is turned up high enough to be audible.**

b. **Verify that the volume within Windows isn't muted or set too low.**

c. **Make sure the speaker cable is connected to the speakers and to the appropriate port on the computer's sound card.**

d. **Update the speaker drivers.**

e. **Check the configuration of the sound card.**

f. **Try the speakers on a known good sound card.** If the speakers work, **replace the failed sound card on the computer.** If the speakers don't work, **replace the failed speakers.**

Check Your Knowledge

1. How would you go about initially troubleshooting a lack of sound coming from a user's computer?

_____

_____

2. A user complains that the microphone is recording at a very low level. How can you troubleshoot this issue?

_____

_____

3. What steps would you take when performing in-depth troubleshooting of a lack of audio from a user's computer?

_____

_____

_____

_____

_____

LAB 6-1

Maintaining and Troubleshooting Peripheral Components

Activity Time: 40 minutes

Scenario:

 You can find a suggested solution for this activity in the \Solutions\Maintaining and Troubleshooting Peripheral Components.txt file in the data file location.

---

1. **Identify the symptoms of the problems.**

---

2. **Diagnose the causes of the problems.**

---

3. **Resolve the problems.**

---

4. **Test to verify the components are functioning properly.**

---

7 | Troubleshooting System Components

Activities included in this chapter:

- Exercise 7-1 Troubleshooting Hard Drive Problems
- Exercise 7-2 Troubleshooting Floppy Drive Problems
- Exercise 7-3 Troubleshooting Optical Drive Problems
- Exercise 7-4 Troubleshooting Power Supplies
- Exercise 7-5 Troubleshooting Memory
- Exercise 7-6 Discussing CPU Troubleshooting
- Exercise 7-7 Troubleshooting System Boards
- Lab 7-1 Troubleshooting System Components

EXERCISE 7-1

Troubleshooting Hard Drive Problems

Scenario:
In this activity, you will troubleshoot hard drive problems.

 There is a simulated version of this activity available on the CD-ROM that shipped with this course. You can run this simulation on any Windows computer to review the activity after class, or as an alternative to performing the activity as a group in class. The activity simulation can be launched either directly from the CD-ROM by clicking the Interactives link and navigating to the appropriate one, or from the installed data file location by opening the C:\085820Data\Simulations\Lesson#\Activity# folder and double-clicking the executable (.exe) file.

What You Do	How You Do It

A Computer Cannot Boot

1. **Diagnose and correct the problem** when a computer cannot boot and the user sees an error message at POST.

   a. **Perform a cold boot.**

   b. **Verify that CMOS lists the correct drive settings.**

   c. **Listen to the drive or touch the drive to determine if it is spinning during POST.**

   d. **Using your multimeter, verify that power connection readings are +12v for Pin 1 and +5v for Pin 4.** Pins 2 and 3 should be grounded.

   e. **Verify that data cable is correctly oriented.**

   f. **Check drive settings:**
      - PATA: Master, slave, or cable select
      - SCSI: Termination and device ID

   g. If nothing else corrects the problem, **replace the drive.**

2. **Test that the drive now works.**

    a. **Boot the system.**

    b. **Verify that you can read and write to the drive you repaired.**

A Second Hard Drive Isn't Recognized

3. **You have installed a second hard drive and it is not recognized. You know that one of the things you need to check when a newly installed drive isn't recognized is the CMOS settings for the drive. What in particular do you need to check in CMOS for this problem?**

---

4. **Another thing you should check when a second hard drive isn't recognized is that the drive was installed correctly. What exactly would you be checking?**

---

5. **A second hard drive was properly installed but you cannot access it by its drive letter. What should your next step be?**

Hard Drive Data Access Problems

6. A user is encountering the following problem: Her computer boots fine and everything works until the user tries to access data on the second hard drive, the D drive. The message "Can't Access This Drive" is displayed when she tries to access the D drive. The user would also like an explanation about what the error message means. List some of the steps you might take to resolve this problem.

7. When a user tries to access the hard drive containing his data, the system locks up and makes a clicking sound. From the DOS prompt, he can change to drive D, but when he tries to access a file or list the files on the drive, it locks up and begins clicking again. What steps might you take to attempt to resolve this problem? What is the most likely cause of the problem?

8. A user reports that some of his folders have begun disappearing and some folder and file names are scrambled with strange characters in their names. What steps might you take to attempt to resolve this problem? What is the most likely cause of the problem?

Wrong Drive Size Reported

9. **A 30-GB hard drive was installed, but the system reports that the drive is about 500 MB. What can be done to resolve this problem?**

10. **A user is questioning the difference between the sizes in GB and bytes. Why is there such a big difference? The disk reports in some places as 9.33 GB and in others as 10,025,000,960 bytes. Why isn't it 10 GB?**

Check Your Knowledge

1. What steps would you take when troubleshooting a boot failure?

2. How would you troubleshoot a second drive not being recognized?

3. What could be the cause of a hard drive producing a clicking sound when accessed?

4. A user reports that there is data corruption on his hard drive, causing some files to become inaccessible. How would you troubleshoot this situation?

EXERCISE 7-2

Troubleshooting Floppy Drive Problems

Activity Time: 20 minutes

Scenario:

Users have opened trouble calls with the help center for the following problems that are related to the floppy drives on their systems.

Ticket No.	Location	User Name	Issue
235001	Main building, 23D41	Angharad Phatek	When the user attempts to access the floppy drive, he sees the message This Disk Is Not Formatted. Do You Want To Format It Now Or Insert Disk Now?
235002	Main building, 32G37	Gary Toomey	The user cannot write to a disk in the floppy drive.
235003	Elmwood Place, cube 37	Zoe Isaacs	When trying to access the floppy drive from the command prompt, she sees the message The System Cannot Find The Drive Specified.
235004	Elmwood Place, cube 42	Etta Romero	User received a floppy disk containing important information from another user. When Etta tries to access the disk through Windows Explorer, she receives a message that the disk is not formatted.

 There is a simulated version of this activity available on the CD-ROM that shipped with this course. You can run this simulation on any Windows computer to review the activity after class, or as an alternative to performing the activity as a group in class. The activity simulation can be launched either directly from the CD-ROM by clicking the Interactives link and navigating to the appropriate one, or from the installed data file location by opening the C:\085820Data\Simulations\Lesson#\Activity# folder and double-clicking the executable (.exe) file.

1. Identify some issues you should check in resolving trouble ticket 235001.

2. List the issues to check in resolving trouble ticket 235002.

3. What might cause the user to receive the error message shown in trouble ticket 235003?

4. What would you recommend to the user to resolve trouble ticket 235004?

Check Your Knowledge

1. When attempting to access a floppy disk, what could cause the error message This Disk Is Not Formatted. Do You Want To Format It Now Or Insert Disk Now?

2. What could cause a disk readable in another system to be unreadable in a user's system?

_____

_____

_____

EXERCISE 7-3

Troubleshooting Optical Drive Problems

Scenario:

The following are the trouble tickets related to CD-ROM, CD-R/RW, DVD, and DVD-R drives that have been assigned to you for resolution.

Ticket No.	Location	User Name	Issue
232001	Main building, 31A57	Nichole Lombard	The door will not open on the CD-ROM drive. The user needs the CD that is in the drive.
232002	Main building, 41A23	Ruth Dalton	User needs to be able to listen to audio CDs. The system reads data and program CDs just fine but there is no audio.
232003	Main building, 11A10	Richard Alston	The user's CD-RW drive was listed as D. A new drive was added to the system and now the D drive does not point to the CD-ROM drive. Some applications cannot find the CD-ROM when he attempts to run the application, even though the CD is in the drive.
232004	Main building, 12D52	Mark Glick	User needs to burn a CD and the drive keeps ejecting the CD media before he can write the disc.
232005	Elmwood Place, cube 7	Jennifer Kulp	The user needs to be able to watch DVDs on her system. She can read CDs, play audio CDs, and read data DVDs in the drive, but does not see any video.

There is a simulated version of this activity available on the CD-ROM that shipped with this course. You can run this simulation on any Windows computer to review the activity after class, or as an alternative to performing the activity as a group in class. The activity simulation can be launched either directly from the CD-ROM by clicking the Interactives link and navigating to the appropriate one, or from the installed data file location by opening the C:\085820Data\Simulations\Lesson#\Activity# folder and double-clicking the executable (.exe) file.

What You Do	How You Do It
1. Resolve trouble ticket 232001.	a. Verify that there is power to the drive.
	b. Press the Eject button on the drive.
	c. Verify that no applications are attempting to read from the CD-ROM.
	d. Open My Computer. Right-click the CD-ROM drive icon and choose Eject.
	e. Straighten out a small paper clip, and then insert the end into the hole on the front of the CD-ROM drive.

2. Resolve trouble ticket 232002.

a. **Verify that you can read a data CD.**

b. **Verify that the speakers are connected properly to the sound card.**

c. **Verify that the speakers are properly powered and turned on.**

d. **Verify that the volume is turned up on the physical speakers.**

e. In the System Tray, **right-click the Volume icon and choose Open Volume Controls.**

f. **Verify that Volume Control is not all the way down and that Mute is not checked.**

g. **Play a system sound such as the Asterisk.**

h. **Verify that the proper sound device drivers are installed.**

i. **Verify that the audio drive is the default sound playback device.**

j. In the Sounds And Audio Devices window, **click the Hardware tab and then click Troubleshoot. Follow the prompts in the Troubleshooting Wizard to attempt to resolve the problem.**

k. **Open the Windows Media Player and attempt to play the default song.**

l. **Verify that the audio cable inside the case that connects the CD-ROM to the sound card is properly installed and that there are no broken wires.**

m. **Verify that you can now play the audio CD.**

3. Regarding trouble ticket 232003, explain to the user what the reason for the problem is and what needs to be done to correct it.

4. What would you suggest that the user try in resolving trouble ticket 232004?

5. After checking over the hardware for the DVD drive on the system, you find no problems. What else might the problem be in trouble ticket 232005?

Check Your Knowledge

1. How can you remove a CD or DVD from a drive that is powered down?

2. What could cause the lack of audio on a CD-ROM drive that can read data just fine?

3. What is needed to be able to play DVD movies on a computer system with a DVD-ROM drive?

    _____

    _____

EXERCISE 7-4

Troubleshooting Power Supplies

Setup:
Before you begin this activity, shut down your computer.

Scenario:
The following are the trouble tickets related to power problems that have been assigned for you to resolve.

Ticket No.	Location	User Name	Issue
125001	Elmwood Place, cube 20	Sylvania Rawleigh	One of the other hardware technicians has been trying to troubleshoot a power problem. The system will not come on when the user turns on the power switch. He determined that the user has an ATX system board and power supply. You have been assigned to take over this trouble ticket.
125002	Main building, 51B24	Darlene Burley	When the user turns on the PC, it doesn't always come on and sometimes it just shuts itself down abruptly, with no warning. When she turns on the system again, there is no fan noise. She is using a legacy database application and the data is being corrupted during the improper shutdowns.
125003	Main building, 21K37	Earle Washburn	The user turns on the power switch, but the system does not come on. He does not hear the fan, there is no power light on, and he hears no beeps or other sounds coming from the system. His system is plugged into a surge protector.

 There is a simulated version of this activity available on the CD-ROM that shipped with this course. You can run this simulation on any Windows computer to review the activity after class, or as an alternative to performing the activity as a group in class. The activity simulation can be launched either directly from the CD-ROM by clicking the Interactives link and navigating to the appropriate one, or from the installed data file location by opening the C:\085820Data\Simulations\Lesson#\Activity# folder and double-clicking the executable (.exe) file.

What You Do	How You Do It
1. Resolve trouble ticket 125001.	a. Set the multimeter for DC volts over 12V.
	b. Locate an available internal power supply connector. If none are free, power off the system and unplug it, then remove one from a floppy drive or CD drive, then power on the system again.
	c. Insert the black probe from the multimeter into one of the two center holes on the internal power supply connector.
	d. Insert the red probe from the multimeter into the hole for the red wire.
	e. Verify that the multimeter reading is +5V DC.
	f. Move the red probe into the hole for the yellow wire.
	g. Verify that the multimeter reading is +12V DC.
	h. Check the documentation for the ATX motherboard to see if there is a logic circuit switch that signals power to be turned on or off, that it is properly connected, and how it should be set.
	i. Verify that the motherboard, processor, memory and video card are all correctly installed and working.

2. What would you do to resolve trouble ticket 125002?

3. If the computer did not start, what would your next action be?

4.   **List the steps you would use to resolve trouble ticket 125003.**

5.   **If the computer did not start, what would your next action be?**

Check Your Knowledge

1.   How can you use a multimeter to troubleshoot power supply problems?

2.   What could cause a power supply to shut down unexpectedly?

3.   Can a surge protector cause a power failure?

EXERCISE 7-5

Troubleshooting Memory

Scenario:

The following are the trouble tickets to which you have been assigned. All of the users are experiencing some type of problem related to the memory installed in their systems.

Ticket No.	Location	User Name	Issue
401001	Main building, 12B52	Roger Wheaton	The user is experiencing corrupted data in his database application. The hard drive has been checked and no problems were found with it. The application was reinstalled and the database was reindexed and all data problems have been corrected. No other users are experiencing this problem when they enter data. He has been successfully entering data until just recently.
401002	Elmwood Place, cube 6	Rory Waldon	The user is complaining of application crashes. He is fine if he is only running his email and word processing programs. If he also opens his graphics program at the same time, then the applications are crashing.
401003	Main building, 22G42	Hazel Beech	Additional memory was installed in her system and now it won't boot.

 There is a simulated version of this activity available on the CD-ROM that shipped with this course. You can run this simulation on any Windows computer to review the activity after class, or as an alternative to performing the activity as a group in class. The activity simulation can be launched either directly from the CD-ROM by clicking the Interactives link and navigating to the appropriate one, or from the installed data file location by opening the C:\085820Data\Simulations\Lesson#\Activity# folder and double-clicking the executable (.exe) file.

1. **After troubleshooting trouble ticket 401001, you have discovered symptoms of a memory problem. What could cause sudden memory problems?**

   a) New virus

   b) Power loss

   c) New memory not compatible

   d) Power surge

2. **You are attempting to resolve trouble ticket 401002. Why is the user only experiencing the problem when additional applications are opened?**

    a) There is not enough memory in the system.

    b) Memory errors are occurring in higher memory than is normally used.

    c) The memory modules are incompatible with one another.

3. **Resolve trouble ticket 401003 by placing the steps in the proper order.**

    Verify that the correct memory was installed in the system.

    Check to see if the BIOS manufacturer has released any upgrades that would resolve the problem.

    Try swapping memory around in the memory banks.

    Verify that memory was installed and configured correctly.

Check Your Knowledge

1. When troubleshooting memory problems, what steps can you take to verify if defective memory is the culprit?

    _____

    _____

    _____

2. How would you troubleshoot a problem with new memory not being recognized, either partially or fully?

    _____

    _____

EXERCISE 7-6

Discussing CPU Troubleshooting

Scenario:

You are attempting to resolve problems for a user who has been reporting intermittent but severe system errors such as frequent unexpected shutdowns. The problems have been getting more frequent, and you have been unable to pinpoint a cause within the system software, power supply, memory, or any adapter cards. You are starting to suspect that there is a bad CPU, and you need to proceed accordingly to get the user back to work with as little downtime and cost as possible.

1. **What initial steps should you take to identify and resolve a potential CPU problem?**

    a) Replace the CPU with a known good processor.

    b) Verify that the CPU fan and other cooling systems are installed and functional.

    c) Replace the system board.

    d) Reseat the CPU.

    e) If the CPU is overclocked, throttle it down to the manufacturer-rated clock speed.

2. **All other diagnostic and corrective steps have failed. You need to verify that it is the CPU itself that is defective. What should you do?**

    a) Replace the system board.

    b) Reinstall the operating system.

    c) Remove all the adapter cards.

    d) Replace the CPU with a known good chip.

Check Your Knowledge

1. When troubleshooting CPU problems, what are key concerns that should be verified first?

    _____

    _____

    _____

2. All your troubleshooting efforts lead you to believe that the CPU is bad. How can you determine with any certainty if the CPU is in fact bad?

    _____

    _____

    _____

EXERCISE 7-7

Troubleshooting System Boards

Scenario:

The following list of trouble tickets are system board problems that you have been assigned to resolve.

Ticket No.	Location	User Name	Issue
135095	Main building. 51B24	Jennifer Bules	When the user turns on the PC, it doesn't always come on and sometimes it just shuts itself down abruptly, with no warning. When she turns on the system again, there is no fan noise. Her data is becoming corrupted from the frequent reboots.
135096	Main building, 21K37	Edward Wever	When the user turns on the computer, he sees a message stating that the computer's date and time are incorrect. He must reset this information in the computer's BIOS each time he starts the computer.
135097	Elmwood Place, cube 20	Sarah Wesson	One of the other hardware technicians has been trying to troubleshoot a power problem. The computer periodically and randomly reboots. The other technician has determined that the user has an ATX system board and power supply. You have been assigned to take over this trouble ticket.

1. What should you do to resolve trouble ticket 135095?

2. What should you do to resolve trouble ticket 135096?

3. **What should you do to resolve trouble ticket 135097?**

Check Your Knowledge

1. How can you resolve a recurring issue in which the time and date keep resetting to a default date and time?

2. What are some of the precautions you need to take when handling a system board?

LAB 7-1

Troubleshooting System Components

Activity Time: 1 hour(s)

Scenario:

 You can find a suggested solution for this activity in the \Solutions\Troubleshooting System Components.txt file in the data file location.

1. Identify the symptoms of the problems.

2. Diagnose the causes of the problems.

3. Resolve the problems.

4. Test to verify the components are functioning properly.

8 | Installing and Configuring Operating Systems

Activities included in this chapter:

- Exercise 8-1 Installing Windows XP Home
- Exercise 8-2 Exploring the Windows XP Home Interface
- Exercise 8-3 Upgrading Windows XP Home to Windows XP Professional
- Exercise 8-4 Creating and Managing Local User Accounts
- Exercise 8-5 Installing Hardware Manually
- Exercise 8-6 Configuring Driver Signing Verification
- Exercise 8-7 Examining Startup Settings
- Exercise 8-8 Viewing Windows Temporary Files
- Exercise 8-9 Configuring Virtual Memory
- Exercise 8-10 Disabling the Remote Registry Service
- Lab 8-1 Configuring and Optimizing a Windows XP Professional System

EXERCISE 8-1

Installing Windows XP Home

Setup:

You will install Windows XP Home on your existing system as if there were no operating system present. Your instructor will provide you with the installation CD-ROM. Your computer system is configured so that the CD-ROM drive is the primary boot device. You have a unique two-digit classroom number.

Scenario:

You have built a custom computer system for a client's home using individual hardware components. You now need to install an operating system. Because this client only needs the system for private home use, you think that Windows XP Home is the operating system choice that will best meet his requirements.

There is a simulated version of this activity available on the CD-ROM that shipped with this course. You can run this simulation on any Windows computer to review the activity after class, or as an alternative to performing the activity as a group in class. The activity simulation can be launched either directly from the CD-ROM by clicking the Interactives link and navigating to the appropriate one, or from the installed data file location by opening the C:\085820Data\Simulations\Lesson#\Activity# folder and double-clicking the executable (.exe) file.

What You Do	How You Do It
1. **Run the Windows XP Home setup program.**	a. **Insert the Windows XP Home installation CD-ROM in your CD-ROM drive.**
	b. **Choose Start→Turn Off Computer.**
	c. **Click Restart.**
	d. When prompted, **press any key on the keyboard to boot from the CD-ROM drive.**
	e. The first part of Setup proceeds in text mode. **Observe as the system detects the basic hardware and loads files for Setup.**

2.   Partition and format the disk.

a.   On the Welcome to Setup screen, **press Enter.**

b.   To accept the license agreement, **press F8.**

c.   You will delete the existing partition. With the C partition selected, **press D.**

d.   To confirm the deletion, **press Enter and then press L.**

e.   To create a partition, **press C.**

f.   **Press the Backspace key to delete the existing value for the partition size.**

g.   **Type** *6000* **and then press Enter.**

h.   To set up Windows in the new partition, **press Enter.**

i.   **Select Format The Partition Using The NTFS File System (Quick) and press Enter.**

j.   **Observe as the format proceeds, the system copies files, and the system restarts.**

Do not boot from the CD-ROM once the setup files have been copied to the hard disk. If you do, you will start the text mode of Setup over again.

3. **Use the Setup Wizard to select installation options.**

a. The system restarts in graphic mode and the first stages of the installation proceed without user intervention. When the Windows XP Home Edition Setup Wizard launches, on the Regional and Language page, to accept the default settings, **click Next.**

b. On the Personalize Your Software page, in the Name box, **type *Software Manager*** and in the Organization box, **type *Information Technology***

c. **Click Next.**

d. On the Your Product Key page, **enter your product key and click Next.**

e. On the What's Your Computer's Name page, **type *Client##* and click Next.**

f. On the Date And Time Settings page, **verify the date and time, select your time zone, and click Next.**

g. The Wizard will pause, installation will proceed, and the Wizard will reappear. On the Networking Settings page, **verify that Typical Settings is selected and click Next.**

4. Complete the post-installation steps.

a. The system will restart in Windows. If prompted to adjust your screen resolution, **click OK twice.**

b. On the Welcome To Microsoft Windows screen, **click Next.**

c. On the Checking Your Internet Connectivity Screen, **click Skip.**

d. If Service Pack 2 is slipstreamed into your Windows XP installation files, on the Help Protect Your PC screen, **select Not Right Now and click Next.**

e. On the Ready To Activate Windows screen, **select No, Remind Me Every Few Days and click Next.**

f. On the Who Will Use This Computer screen, in the Your Name box, **type** *Admin##* **and click Next.**

g. **Click Finish.**

h. **Remove the installation CD-ROM from the drive.**

---

5. What additional steps should you perform at this point to complete the installation?

   a) Create additional user accounts.

   b) Install applications.

   c) Install Service Packs and other critical updates.

   d) Install a printer.

---

6.   **Verify the installation.**

    a.   The system will automatically log you on as the Admin## user. The Start menu will open. From the Start menu, **right-click My Computer, and choose Manage.**

    b.   In Computer Management, under System Tools, **select Device Manager.**

    c.   **Expand each of the hardware categories and verify that there are no devices displayed with Error or Warning icons.**

    d.   **Close Computer Management.**

7.   **Create a password for your user account.**

    a.   **Choose Start→Control Panel.**

    b.   **Click User Accounts.**

    c.   **Click the Admin## account.**

    d.   **Click Create A Password.**

    e.   **Type and confirm *!Pass1234* and click Create Password.**

    f.   **Click Yes, Make Private.**

    g.   **Close User Accounts and Control Panel.**

Check Your Knowledge

1.   When installing Windows XP, is an Internet connection necessary?

2.   How can you obtain Windows updates via the Internet?

3. What is the purpose of Windows Genuine Advantage (WGA) validation?

    _____

    _____

    _____

4. Is product activation necessary or can Windows be used without activation?

    _____

EXERCISE 8-2

Exploring the Windows XP Home Interface

Scenario:

You have just installed Windows XP Home. Previously you worked mostly with Windows XP Professional, and you want to identify some of the areas where the two operating systems are different.

 There is a simulated version of this activity available on the CD-ROM that shipped with this course. You can run this simulation on any Windows computer to review the activity after class, or as an alternative to performing the activity as a group in class. The activity simulation can be launched either directly from the CD-ROM by clicking the Interactives link and navigating to the appropriate one, or from the installed data file location by opening the C:\085820Data\Simulations\Lesson#\Activity# folder and double-clicking the executable (.exe) file.

What You Do	How You Do It
1. **Identify user interface differences between Windows XP Home and Windows XP Professional.**	a. **Choose Start.**
	b. By default, The Start menu arrangement is slightly different. There is no My Recent Documents link and no Printers and Faxes link. **Click My Computer.**
	c. By default, the Address bar is not displayed. **Choose Tools→Folder Options.**
	d. **Click the View tab.**
	e. **Scroll to the bottom of the Advanced Settings list.**
	f. There is no option to turn off Simple File Sharing. **Click Cancel.**
	g. **Right-click the C drive and choose Properties.**
	h. There is no Security tab. You cannot see or modify the NTFS permissions on the drive. **Click Cancel.**
	i. **Close My Computer.**

Check Your Knowledge

1. What are some of the differences between Windows XP Professional and Windows XP Home editions?

_____

_____

_____

EXERCISE 8-3

Upgrading Windows XP Home to Windows XP Professional

Setup:

Your instructor will provide you with the Windows XP Professional installation CD-ROM. If Service Pack 2 is not slipstreamed into your Windows XP Professional installation source, your instructor will provide you with the Service Pack 2 CD-ROM as well.

Scenario:

A customer purchased a computer that came preinstalled with Windows XP Home, but after using it for a while, the customer has decided that she prefers to use the more advanced functionality of Windows XP Professional. The computer system vendor has provided an installation CD for Windows XP Professional, and the customer would like you to upgrade her system.

 There is a simulated version of this activity available on the CD-ROM that shipped with this course. You can run this simulation on any Windows computer to review the activity after class, or as an alternative to performing the activity as a group in class. The activity simulation can be launched either directly from the CD-ROM by clicking the Interactives link and navigating to the appropriate one, or from the installed data file location by opening the C:\085820Data\Simulations\Lesson#\Activity# folder and double-clicking the executable (.exe) file.

What You Do	How You Do It
1. **Run the Microsoft Windows Setup Advisor.**	a. **Insert the Windows XP Professional Installation CD-ROM.**
	b. The Setup program should launch automatically. **Click Check System Compatibility.**
	c. **Click Check My System Automatically.**
	d. **Select, No, Skip This Step And Continue Installing Windows and click Next.**

e. There should be no incompatibilities. **Click Finish.**

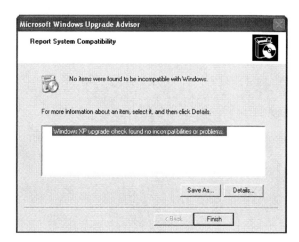

f. In the Windows XP Setup program, **click Back.**

2. **Run the Windows XP Professional upgrade program.**

a. **Click Install Windows XP.**

b. **Verify that the Installation Type is Upgrade (Recommended) and click Next.**

c. **Select I Accept This Agreement and click Next.**

d. On the Your Product Key page, **type your product key and click Next.**

e. To save time at this point in the installation, **select No, Skip This Step And Continue Installing Windows and click Next.**

3. **Complete the post-installation steps.**

a. The system will restart, load the Windows XP Professional Setup program, and Setup will continue. The installation program might reload more than once. When the upgrade is complete, the system will restart in Windows. On the Welcome To Microsoft Windows screen, **click Next.**

 Do not boot from the CD-ROM when the system restarts. If you do, you will start Setup over again.

b. If Service Pack 2 is slipstreamed into your Windows XP installation files, on the Help Protect Your PC screen, **select Not Right Now and click Next.**

c. On the Ready To Activate Windows screen, **select No, Remind Me Every Few Days and click Next.**

d. **Click Finish.**

e. **Remove the installation CD-ROM.**

4. If Service Pack 2 is not slipstreamed into your Windows installation, **install Service Pack 2.**

a. To log on as your Admin## account, in the Password field, **type !Pass1234 and press Enter.**

b. **Insert the Windows XP Service Pack 2 CD-ROM.**

c. The Service Pack 2 installation should run automatically. **Click Continue.**

d. **Click Install Now.**

e. In the Windows XP Service Pack 2 Setup Wizard, **click Next.**

f. **Select I Agree and click Next.**

g. To accept the uninstall folder location, **click Next.**

h. When the installation is complete, **click Finish.**

i. The system will restart. On the Help Protect Your PC screen, **select Not Right Now and click Next.**

j. To log on as your Admin## account, **type !Pass1234 and press Enter.**

k. The Windows Security Center window will open. **Close the Windows Security Center.**

5. If your Windows system has been activated, **update the system from Windows Update.**

a. **Choose Start→All Programs→Windows Update.**

b. If prompted to install Windows Update software, **click Install, and then click Install Now.**

c. To see the list of available and recommended updates, **click Custom.**

d. If an Internet Explorer dialog box appears, **verify that the In The Future, Do Not Show This Message check box is checked and click Yes.**

e. If prompted to install the latest version of Windows Update, **click Download And Install Now.**

f. When the installation is complete, **click Restart Now.**

g. **Log in as your Admin## account.**

h. **Choose Start→All Programs→Windows Update.**

i. To see the list of available and recommended updates broken down by category, **click Custom.**

j. To review optional software updates, under Select By Type, **click the Software, Optional link.**

k. To review optional hardware updates, under Select By Type, **click the Hardware, Optional link.**

l. **Click the High Priority link.**

m. All high-priority updates should be selected by default. **Click Review And Install Updates. Click Install Updates.**

n. **Follow any prompts or dialog boxes and restart the system as necessary.**

6. Verify the installation.

    a. **Choose Start, right-click My Computer, and choose Manage.**

    b. **In Computer Management, under System Tools, select Device Manager.**

    c. **Expand each of the hardware categories and verify that there are no devices displayed with Error or Warning icons.**

    d. **Close Computer Management.**

Check Your Knowledge

1. What is the purpose of the Microsoft Windows Setup Advisor?

2. When installing Windows XP Professional, should you install available service packs or run Windows Update?

EXERCISE 8-4

Creating and Managing Local User Accounts

Setup:
There are two administrative user accounts on the computer: the default Administrator account and an account named Admin## that you created when you installed Windows.

Scenario:
You have been called in to configure a client's new Windows XP computer. After interviewing the client, you've determined that she needs accounts on the computer for the following users:

● Susan Williams (the client)

● Jeff Bernard (Susan's employee in her home-based business)

For consistency, you recommend that your client use the following naming convention for user accounts: the user's first name plus the first initial of his or her last name. In addition, you recommend that each user have a reasonably complex password. Susan does not want her employee to be able to change his password. Because Susan is the owner of the computer, you plan to add her account to the Administrators group.

 There is a simulated version of this activity available on the CD-ROM that shipped with this course. You can run this simulation on any Windows computer to review the activity after class, or as an alternative to performing the activity as a group in class. The activity simulation can be launched either directly from the CD-ROM by clicking the Interactives link and navigating to the appropriate one, or from the installed data file location by opening the C:\ 085820Data\Simulations\Lesson#\Activity# folder and double-clicking the executable (.exe) file.

What You Do	How You Do It
1. Create the local accounts.	a. **Open Computer Management.**
	b. **Expand Local Users And Groups.**
	c. **Select the Users folder.**
	d. **Choose Action→New User.**
	e. In the User Name text box, **type *SusanW***

f. In the Full Name text box, **type** *Susan Williams*

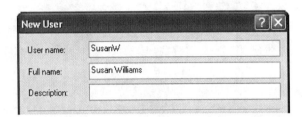

g. In the Password text box, **type** *!Pass1234*

h. In the Confirm Password text box, **type** *!Pass1234*

i. **Uncheck the User Must Change Password At Next Logon check box.**

j. **Click Create.**

k. **Enter the account information for the user Jeff Bernard.**

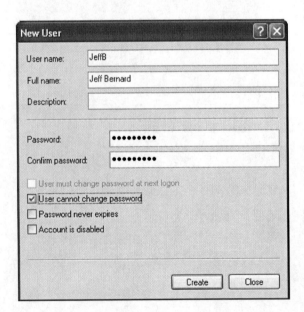

l. **Click Create.**

	m. **Click Close.**

2. **Add SusanW to the built-in Administrators group.**	a. **Select the Groups folder.**
	b. **Double-click the Administrators group.**
	c. **Click Add.**
	d. **Type *SusanW* and then click OK.**
	e. To close the Administrators Properties dialog box, **click OK.**
	f. **Close Computer Management.**

3. **Verify that you can log on as SusanW.**	a. **Choose Start→Log Off.**
	b. **Click Log Off.**
	c. **Click Susan Williams.**
	d. In the Password text box, **type *!Pass1234***
	e. **Press Enter.**
	f. **Log off and log back on as Admin##.**

Check Your Knowledge

1. How can you add additional users to a computer running Windows XP?

_____

_____

_____

2. Can you give a user additional privileges in Windows XP?

_____

_____

_____

EXERCISE 8-5

Installing Hardware Manually

Scenario:

You have a desktop computer with a single network adapter, but you need to do some testing on the system as if it had two network adapters. You decide to install The Microsoft Loopback Adapter, which is a software interface that can simulate the presence of a network adapter.

 There is a simulated version of this activity available on the CD-ROM that shipped with this course. You can run this simulation on any Windows computer to review the activity after class, or as an alternative to performing the activity as a group in class. The activity simulation can be launched either directly from the CD-ROM by clicking the Interactives link and navigating to the appropriate one, or from the installed data file location by opening the C:\ 085820Data\Simulations\Lesson#\Activity# folder and double-clicking the executable (.exe) file.

What You Do	How You Do It
1. **Install the Microsoft Loopback Adapter.**	a. **Choose Start→Control Panel.**
	b. **Click Printers And Other Hardware.**
	c. To run the Add Hardware Wizard, in the Task Pane, **click Add Hardware.**
	d. **Click Next.**
	e. The wizard searches for new hardware. **Select Yes, I Have Already Connected The Hardware and click Next.**

f. **Drag the scroll box to the bottom of the Installed Hardware list and select Add A New Hardware Device. Click Next.**

g. **Select Install The Hardware That I Manually Select From A List. Click Next.**

h. **Scroll down to select Network Adapters. Click Next.**

i. In the Network Adapter list, **select Microsoft Loopback Adapter. Click Next.**

j. This is an adapter driver that you can install without manufacturer's driver files. To install the hardware, **click Next.**

k. **Click Finish.**

2. **Verify the device installation.**

a. In the Task Pane, **click System.**

b. **Click the Hardware tab and click Device Manager.**

c. In Device Manager, **expand the Network Adapters category.**

d. Both the adapters are listed. **Close Device Manager.**

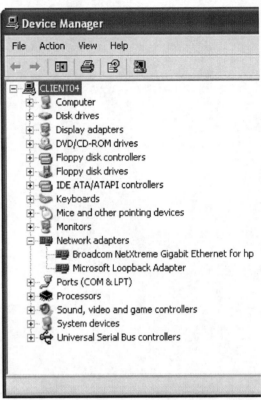

e. In the System Properties dialog box, **click Cancel.**

f. **Close the Printers And Other Hardware window.**

Check Your Knowledge

1. How do you manually add new hardware in Windows XP?

EXERCISE 8-6

Configuring Driver Signing Verification

Scenario:

You work in a lightly managed Windows XP Professional environment. Users have a lot of autonomy and occasionally make changes to the hardware configurations of their own systems. To protect your environment, you first want to make sure that all the current drivers on each user's computer are safe. Then, you want to make sure that users cannot install any hardware with unsigned device drivers.

 There is a simulated version of this activity available on the CD-ROM that shipped with this course. You can run this simulation on any Windows computer to review the activity after class, or as an alternative to performing the activity as a group in class. The activity simulation can be launched either directly from the CD-ROM by clicking the Interactives link and navigating to the appropriate one, or from the installed data file location by opening the C:\085820Data\Simulations\Lesson#\Activity# folder and double-clicking the executable (.exe) file.

What You Do	How You Do It
1. **Determine the signing status of current system and driver files.**	a. **Choose Start→Run.**
	b. **Type** *sigverif* **and click OK.**
	c. **Click Advanced.**
	d. Use this dialog box to verify the files that will be included in the scan. You could also set logging options in this dialog box. **Click OK.**

e. **Click Start.**

f. The system builds a list of files and then scans the selected files. This takes a few moments. If you had any unsigned files, a results window would appear listing the files. This information is also logged to the Sigverif.txt log file. To close the message box and return to the File Signature Verification dialog box, **click OK.**

g. If any unsigned drivers are reported, make a note of the driver file names and close the results list. In the File Signature Verification dialog box, **click Close.**

2. **If you discovered any unsigned files during the scan, how would you use this information?**

3. **Configure the system to block the installation of unsigned drivers.**

   a. **Choose Start, right-click My Computer, and choose Properties.**

   b. **Click the Hardware tab.**

   c. On the Hardware page of the System Properties dialog box, **click Driver Signing.**

   d. **Select Block – Never Install Unsigned Driver Software.**

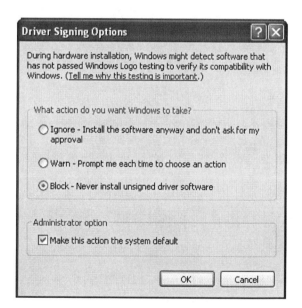

   e. **Click OK twice.**

Check Your Knowledge

1. How can you verify that all drivers and system files are signed?

2. Should any unsigned drivers ever be installed?

_____

_____

_____

3. Is it possible to prevent users from installing unsigned drivers?

_____

_____

_____

EXERCISE 8-7

Examining Startup Settings

Scenario:

In this activity, you will examine the startup settings that are controlled by the Boot.ini file.

 There is a simulated version of this activity available on the CD-ROM that shipped with this course. You can run this simulation on any Windows computer to review the activity after class, or as an alternative to performing the activity as a group in class. The activity simulation can be launched either directly from the CD-ROM by clicking the Interactives link and navigating to the appropriate one, or from the installed data file location by opening the C:\ 085820Data\Simulations\Lesson#\Activity# folder and double-clicking the executable (.exe) file.

What You Do	How You Do It
1. **Examine the current startup settings.**	a. **Choose Start, right-click My Computer, and choose Properties.**
	b. **Click the Advanced tab.**
	c. Under Startup And Recovery, **click Settings.**
	d. If there is more than one operating system installed, you can choose which one will load by default when the system starts up. **Verify that the Default Operating System is Microsoft Windows XP Professional.**

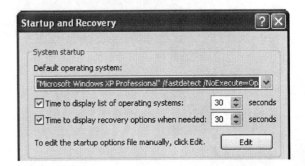

	e. If there were more than one operating system installed, the user would see a list of operating systems and could choose one to load. The list would be displayed for a fixed amount of time before the default operating system loads. **Verify that the Time To Display List Of Operating Systems value is 30 seconds.**

2. Examine the Boot.ini file.

a. **Click Edit.**

b. The settings in the Startup And Recovery dialog box are stored in the Boot.ini file. You could edit the file manually if you chose. **Close Notepad** without saving any changes.

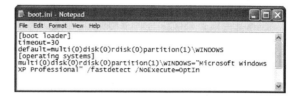

c. To close the Startup And Recovery dialog box and leave the System Properties dialog box open, **click Cancel.**

Check Your Knowledge

1. How can you access current startup settings?

_____

_____

2. What kind of information is stored in the boot.ini file?

_____

_____

EXERCISE 8-8

Viewing Windows Temporary Files

Scenario:

You are unsure where your Windows system stores its temporary files. You would like to find the temporary file storage location and open it to determine if an inordinate number of temporary files has accumulated on the system.

 There is a simulated version of this activity available on the CD-ROM that shipped with this course. You can run this simulation on any Windows computer to review the activity after class, or as an alternative to performing the activity as a group in class. The activity simulation can be launched either directly from the CD-ROM by clicking the Interactives link and navigating to the appropriate one, or from the installed data file location by opening the C:\ 085820Data\Simulations\Lesson#\Activity# folder and double-clicking the executable (.exe) file.

What You Do	How You Do It
1. Determine the value of the Path variable.	a. On the Advanced page of the System Properties dialog box, **click Environment Variables.**
	b. **Verify that the TEMP variable points to the local administrator's user profile.**

c. To view the complete path TEMP variable, **click Edit.**

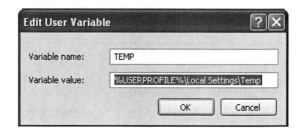

d. **Click Cancel three times.**

2. **View the files in the temporary file storage location.**

a. **Choose Start→My Computer.**

b. **Open the C drive.**

c. If necessary, **click Show the Contents Of This Folder.**

d. **Open the Documents And Settings folder.**

e. **Open the Admin## folder.**

f. The temporary files folder is hidden. **Choose Tools→Folder Options.**

g. **Click the View tab.**

h. In the Advanced Settings list, **select Show Hidden Files And Folders and click OK.**

> Hidden files and folders
> ○ Do not show hidden files and folders
> ◉ Show hidden files and folders

i. **Open the Local Settings folder.**

j. To view temporary files, **open the Temp folder.**

k. **Close the Temp window.**

Check Your Knowledge

1. Where are Windows temporary files stored?

_____

_____

_____

2. You have determined where the temporary files are stored but are unable to navigate to the folder. What could be the problem?

_____

_____

_____

EXERCISE 8-9

Configuring Virtual Memory

Scenario:

You manage Windows XP Professional desktop systems for a group of desktop-publishing specialists who use highly memory-intensive applications for developing, editing, and printing graphics. They have been receiving some low-memory errors. Until you can purchase and install more RAM, you want to ensure that you have adequate pagefile space allocated on your system to meet their virtual memory needs. There is quite a bit of empty space on their hard disks.

 There is a simulated version of this activity available on the CD-ROM that shipped with this course. You can run this simulation on any Windows computer to review the activity after class, or as an alternative to performing the activity as a group in class. The activity simulation can be launched either directly from the CD-ROM by clicking the Interactives link and navigating to the appropriate one, or from the installed data file location by opening the C:\085820Data\Simulations\Lesson#\Activity# folder and double-clicking the executable (.exe) file.

What You Do	How You Do It
1. **Open the Virtual Memory dialog box.**	a. **Choose Start, right-click My Computer, and choose Properties.**
	b. **Click the Advanced tab.**
	c. On the Advanced tab of the System Properties dialog box, under Performance, **click Settings.**
	d. In the Performance Options dialog box, **click the Advanced tab.**

e.   Under Virtual Memory, **click Change.**

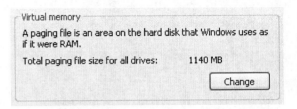

2.   **Adjust the virtual memory settings.**

a.   To select the text, **double-click in the Initial Size text box.**

b.   **Type a value that is 100 MB greater than the existing initial size.**

c.   To select the text, **double-click in the Maximum Size text box.**

d.   **Type a value that is 100 MB greater than the existing initial size.**

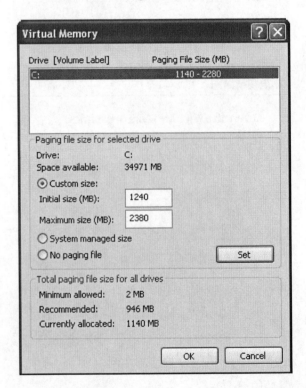

e.   **Click Set.**

f.   **Click OK three times.**

Check Your Knowledge

1. How can you adjust virtual memory settings in Windows XP?

   _____

   _____

2. Are there specific guidelines as to how to properly adjust virtual memory settings?

   _____

   _____

   _____

EXERCISE 8-10

Disabling the Remote Registry Service

Scenario:

You have users who complain that their systems are running slowly and take a long time to start up. You want to improve system performance and the boot time by preventing unnecessary services from loading. After examining the list of running services, you determine that there is no need for administrators to edit the registry on these machines from elsewhere on the network, so you decide that it would be advisable to disable the Remote Registry service.

 There is a simulated version of this activity available on the CD-ROM that shipped with this course. You can run this simulation on any Windows computer to review the activity after class, or as an alternative to performing the activity as a group in class. The activity simulation can be launched either directly from the CD-ROM by clicking the Interactives link and navigating to the appropriate one, or from the installed data file location by opening the C:\ 085820Data\Simulations\Lesson#\Activity# folder and double-clicking the executable (.exe) file.

What You Do	How You Do It
1. Open Computer Management.	a. Choose Start, right-click My Computer, and choose Manage.
	b. Expand Services And Applications and select Services.
2. Disable the service.	a. Scroll the services list to locate the Remote Registry service.
	b. Double-click the Remote Registry service.

c. **Click the Startup Type drop-down arrow and choose Disabled.**

d. **Click Stop.**

e. **Click OK.**

f. **Close Computer Management.**

Check Your Knowledge

1. What is the purpose of disabling a service?

_____

_____

2. How can you disable a service?

_____

_____

_____

_____

LAB 8-1

Configuring and Optimizing a Windows XP Professional System

Activity Time: 20 minutes

Scenario:

 You can find a suggested solution for this activity in the Solutions\Configuring and Optimizing a Windows XP Professional System.txt file in the student data files.

1. Configure the system to warn users about installing unsigned drivers.

2. Install the drivers for the new modem.

3. Create a new 1 GB NTFS Data partition in the unpartitioned space on the primary hard disk.

4. Run Disk Cleanup to remove unneeded files and Windows components from the C drive.

9 Maintaining and Troubleshooting Microsoft Windows

Activities included in this chapter:

- Exercise 9-1 Exploring Disk Management Tools
- Exercise 9-2 Exploring System Management Utilities
- Exercise 9-3 Backing Up System State Data
- Exercise 9-4 Identifying System Errors
- Exercise 9-5 Troubleshooting a Remote Computer with Remote Desktop
- Exercise 9-6 Restoring System State Data
- Exercise 9-7 Restoring the System to a Restore Point
- Exercise 9-8 Recovering the System With Last Known Good
- Exercise 9-9 Testing the Recovery Console
- Exercise 9-10 Creating and Testing a Windows XP Boot Floppy Disk
- Lab 9-1 Preparing for Automated System Recovery (ASR)

EXERCISE 9-1

Exploring Disk Management Tools

Setup:

There are at least two NTFS partitions on the primary hard disk. If you did not do the lab for the *Installing and Configuring Operating Systems* lesson, you will need to create a second NTFS partition.

Scenario:

As a computer support professional, you will be responsible for managing and maintaining hard disk configuration and performance for your customer. To prepare yourself for professional disk-management tasks, you plan to review the status of the disks on your own local system.

 There is a simulated version of this activity available on the CD-ROM that shipped with this course. You can run this simulation on any Windows computer to review the activity after class, or as an alternative to performing the activity as a group in class. The activity simulation can be launched either directly from the CD-ROM by clicking the Interactives link and navigating to the appropriate one, or from the installed data file location by opening the C:\085820Data\Simulations\Lesson#\Activity# folder and double-clicking the executable (.exe) file.

What You Do	How You Do It
1. Check the status of your disk.	a. **Choose Start→All Programs→ Accessories→Command Prompt.**
	b. **Enter** *chkdsk*

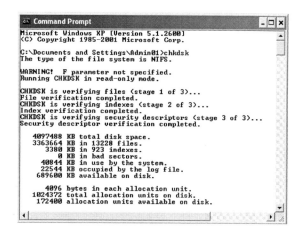

	c. **Examine the chkdsk results and enter** *cls* to clear the screen.
2. Did chkdsk find any bad sectors?	
3. Use diskpart.exe to examine the partitions on your disk.	a. **Enter** *diskpart*
	b. At the DISKPART prompt, to see a list of DISKPART commands, **enter** *help*
	c. **Enter** *list disk*
	d. To move the focus to disk 0, **enter** *select disk 0*
	e. To see details about the disk configuration, **enter** *detail disk*
	f. To exit DISKPART, **enter** *exit*
	g. **Close the Command Prompt window.**

4. **Check the fragmentation status of your disk.**

a. **Choose Start→Control Panel.**

b. **Click Performance And Maintenance.**

c. In the Performance And Maintenance window, under Pick A Task, **click Rearrange Items On Your Hard Disk To Make Programs Run Faster.**

d. The Disk Defragmenter window opens. With the C drive selected, **click Analyze.**

e. When the analysis is complete, a Disk Defragmenter message box appears. In the Disk Defragmenter message box, **click View Report.**

f. To determine the overall fragmentation percentage, in the Volume Information area, **scroll to the Volume Fragmentation statistics.**

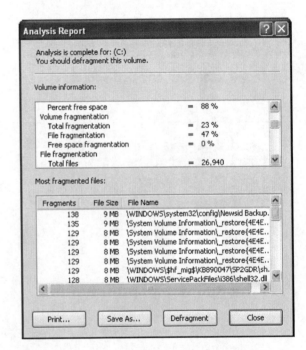

g. To sort the list to determine which files are most fragmented, in the Most Fragmented Files list, **click twice on the Fragments column heading.**

h. To determine whether or not you should defragment, **view the top section of the report. Click Close.**

i. **Close Disk Defragmenter.**

5. **Based on the analysis, should you defragment?**

Check Your Knowledge

1. What is the purpose of the chkdsk tool?

2. What is the purpose of the diskpart tool?

3. Is a third-party tool required to defragment a hard drive in Windows XP?

EXERCISE 9-2

Exploring System Management Utilities

Scenario:

As a computer support professional, you will be responsible for managing and maintaining system configuration and performance for your customers. To prepare yourself for professional system-management tasks, you plan to review the status of the system components on your own local computer.

 There is a simulated version of this activity available on the CD-ROM that shipped with this course. You can run this simulation on any Windows computer to review the activity after class, or as an alternative to performing the activity as a group in class. The activity simulation can be launched either directly from the CD-ROM by clicking the Interactives link and navigating to the appropriate one, or from the installed data file location by opening the C:\ 085820Data\Simulations\Lesson#\Activity# folder and double-clicking the executable (.exe) file.

What You Do	How You Do It
1. View device status in Device Manager.	a. In the Control Panel Performance And Maintenance window, **click System.**
	b. **Click the Hardware tab.**
	c. **Click Device Manager.**
	d. **Expand the Keyboards node.**
	e. **Verify that the keyboard device icon appears normal and double-click the icon to open the keyboard's property sheet.**

	f. **Click the Driver tab.**
	g. You can view details about the driver, update or roll back the driver, or uninstall the device on the Driver page. **Click the Resources tab.**
	h. The Resources page shows the resource settings for the device. It is rare that you would have to adjust resource allocation manually. **Click Cancel.**
	i. **Expand other categories and view the status and properties of other devices.**

      j.   **Close Device Manager.**

      k.   **Close System Properties.**

      l.   **Close Performance And Maintenance.**

2.   **Did any devices have any problems?**

3. **Examine the system status with Task Manager.**

a. **Right-click the taskbar and choose Task Manager.**

b. The Applications page is blank because there are no application windows open. To start an application, **click New Task.**

c. To run Notepad, **type *notepad* and click OK.**

d. Notepad opens in the background and the Notepad task appears on the Applications page. **Verify that a running process count, CPU usage percentage, and committed memory value appear in the Task Manager status bar.**

e. **Verify that the CPU usage gauge appears in the notification area of the taskbar.**

f. In Task Manager, **right-click the Notepad application and choose Go To Process.**

g. There are many processes running on the system. Most are running in the background, not in their own windows, and so they do not appear on the Applications page. To close Notepad, with the Notepad process selected, **click End Process.**

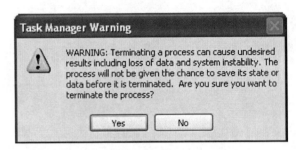

h. **Click Yes.**

i. **Click the Performance tab.**

j. The Performance page provides a graphical report on system performance statistics. **Click the Networking tab.**

k. The Networking tab provides a graphical report on network activity. **Click the Users tab.**

l. When Fast User Switching is enabled, the Users tab is available and shows any users who are currently logged on. **Close Task Manager.**

4. **Examine the system configuration settings with msconfig.**

a. **Choose Start→Help And Support.**

b. Under Pick A Task, **click Use Tools To View Your Computer Information And Diagnose Problems.**

c. In the Tools list, **click System Configuration Utility.**

d. **Click Open System Configuration Utility.**

e. System Configuration is a diagnostic and troubleshooting utility that can help auto-mate routine troubleshooting steps. The General page controls overall startup behavior. **Click the System.ini tab.**

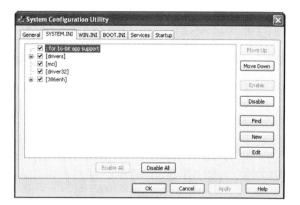

f. System.ini and Win.ini are legacy configu-ration files from earlier DOS shell versions of Windows. Windows will process these files if they are present. You can use Sys-tem Configuration to enable or disable portions of these files. **Click the Boot.ini tab.**

g. System Configuration provides another way to modify the startup settings in Boot.ini. **Click the Services tab.**

h. You can use System Configuration to enable or disable services. **Click the Startup tab.**

i. You can view and manage items that are configured to load at system startup. To close System Configuration, **click Cancel.**

5. **Examine the system information with msinfo32.**

a. In the Help And Support Center, in the Tools list, **click Advanced System Information.**

b. **Click View Detailed System Information (Msinfo32.exe).**

c. **Maximize System Information.**

d. In the System Summary, **verify that the system is running Windows XP Professional with Service Pack 2. Expand Hardware Resources.**

e. You can see the assignments for each category of hardware resources. To view the assigned interrupts, **select IRQs.**

f. **Collapse Hardware Resources.**

g. You can see detailed information about all aspects of the computer system. **Expand Components and select CD-ROM.**

h. **Collapse Components.**

i. **Expand Software Environment and select System Drivers.**

j. **Collapse Software Environment.**

k. **Expand Internet Settings, Internet Explorer.**

l. **Select Summary.**

m. **Close System Information.**

n. **Close the Help And Support Center.**

6.   Review the system logs.

   a.   **Choose Start, right-click My Computer, and choose Manage.**

   b.   Under System Tools, **select Event Viewer.**

   c.   **Double-click the System log.**

   d.   **Double-click the first Information entry in the log.**

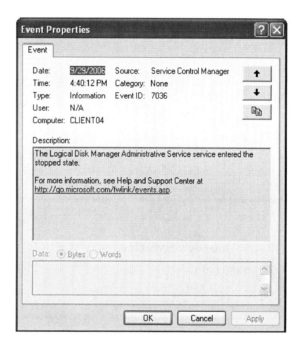

   e.   This shows you the basic structure of an event log entry. In the Event Properties window, **click the Down arrow and then the Up arrow to scroll through the event log entries.**

   f.   To close the Event Properties window, **click Cancel.**

   g.   **Choose View→Filter.**

h. **Uncheck all event types except Warning and Error.**

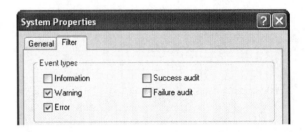

i. **Click OK.**

j. Now the Warning and Error messages, if any, appear in sequence. It's perfectly normal to see a few Error and Warning messages in a log. Most of these problems are either minor or due to some external condition, such as a server being unavailable. **Close Computer Management.**

Check Your Knowledge

1. What kind of information does Device Manager provide?

   _____

   _____

   _____

2. What kind of information does Task Manager provide?

   _____

   _____

   _____

3. What kind of information does msconfig provide?

   _____

   _____

4. What useful information can Event Viewer display?

   _____

   _____

   _____

5. What is msinfo32 and what is it used for?

_____

_____

_____

EXERCISE 9-3

Backing Up System State Data

Setup:

You will need approximately 400 MB of free space on your C drive to complete the backup.

Scenario:

One of your clients uses his computer 100 percent of the time to do his job. His computer uses the Windows XP operating system. He is very concerned about a computer crash. He wants to make sure that you will be able to reconstruct his computer as quickly as possible in the event of an operating system failure.

 There is a simulated version of this activity available on the CD-ROM that shipped with this course. You can run this simulation on any Windows computer to review the activity after class, or as an alternative to performing the activity as a group in class. The activity simulation can be launched either directly from the CD-ROM by clicking the Interactives link and navigating to the appropriate one, or from the installed data file location by opening the C:\085820Data\Simulations\Lesson#\Activity# folder and double-clicking the executable (.exe) file.

What You Do	How You Do It
1. Create a folder for storing the System State data backup.	a. **Open Windows Explorer.**
	b. **Select the C drive.**
	c. **Choose File→Properties.**
	d. **Verify that you have enough free disk space to store the System State data backup.**

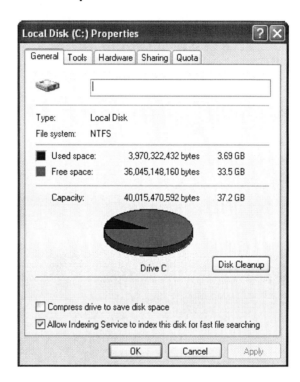

	e. To close the Properties dialog box, **click Cancel.**
	f. **Choose File→New→Folder.**
	g. **Type *Backup* and press Enter.**
	h. **Close Windows Explorer.**

2. Back up the System State data.

a. From the Start menu, **choose All Programs→Accessories→System Tools→Backup.**

b. **Verify that the Always Start In Wizard Mode check box is checked.**

c. **Click Next.**

d. **Verify that Back Up Files And Settings is selected. Click Next.**

e. **Select Let Me Choose What To Back Up and click Next.**

f. Below Items To Back Up, **expand My Computer.**

g. **Check the System State check box.**

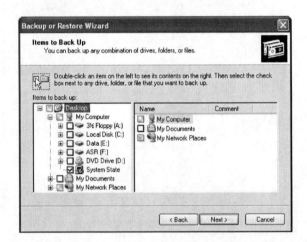

h. **Click Next.**

i. **Click Cancel.** In the Save As dialog box, from the Save In drop-down list, **select Local Disk (C:). Open the Backup folder and click Save.**

j. **Click Next.**

k. **Click Finish.**

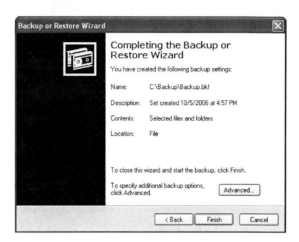

l. When the backup is complete, **click Close.**

Check Your Knowledge

1. What is the principal benefit of backing up System State data?

_____

_____

2. Does Windows XP Backup support back up to CD or DVD media?

_____

3. What is the quickest way of verifying Windows system file integrity?

_____

_____

EXERCISE 9-4

Identifying System Errors

Scenario:
In this activity, you will interpret system errors and discuss possible appropriate responses to error conditions.

1. **A user calls saying that her screen occasionally goes blue and the system shuts down. What should you advise her to do?**

   a) Call the Help Desk the next time the shutdown is in progress.

   b) Reboot manually after the automatic restart.

   c) Record as much information on the top of the blue screen as she can so that you can research the particular error.

   d) Run the system in Safe Mode.

2. **A user reports that his Microsoft Word window has gone blank and he cannot type text. What are possible approaches to resolving his problem?**

   a) Reboot the computer.

   b) Run another copy of Microsoft Word.

   c) Wait a few minutes to see if the application returns to normal.

   d) Use Task Manager to shut down the application if it has a status of Not Responding.

3. **A user reports her monitor display is "fuzzy" and hard to look at. What is a possible cause of this problem?**

   a) Display settings for the monitor are incorrectly configured.

   b) The power cord is unplugged.

   c) The monitor cable is not properly seated.

   d) The monitor device is disabled in Windows.

4. **A user reports that while she is editing a document, she receives an "invalid working directory" message from her application. What is a good diagnostic question to ask in response to this error?**

   a) Did the application work yesterday?

   b) Is anyone else having this problem?

   c) Who installed the application?

   d) Have you deleted any files or folders lately?

5. **Match the error message with its most likely cause.**

___ Invalid boot disk	a. Corrupted device driver
___ Inaccessible boot device	b. POST failure (related to the hard disk)
___ Device failed during startup	c. Non-bootable disk left in the drive
___ Registry file failure	d. Hard disk controller failure
___ Numeric error code 1701	e. Disk problem leading to corrupted hive files

Check Your Knowledge

1. How can you shut down an application that has stopped responding without shutting down the system altogether?

   _____

2. What is the first step to take when troubleshooting a computer's blue screen errors?

   _____

   _____

   _____

3. What should you check first when a computer is reporting an Invalid Boot Disk message on boot?

   _____

4. Device Manager reports a device failed during system startup. What could cause this issue?

   _____

   _____

EXERCISE 9-5

Troubleshooting a Remote Computer with Remote Desktop

Setup:

You are going to work with a partner to complete this activity. You will take turns playing the role of the helper and the user needing assistance. First, the user needing assistance will enable Remote Desktop. Then, the helper will connect to that computer using Remote Desktop Connection and the Administrator user account.

Scenario:

You have been assigned to support a user whose office is several floors away from yours. You would like to be able to troubleshoot this computer without having to go to the user's office.

There is a simulated version of this activity available on the CD-ROM that shipped with this course. You can run this simulation on any Windows computer to review the activity after class, or as an alternative to performing the activity as a group in class. The activity simulation can be launched either directly from the CD-ROM by clicking the Interactives link and navigating to the appropriate one, or from the installed data file location by opening the C:\ 085820Data\Simulations\Lesson#\Activity# folder and double-clicking the executable (.exe) file.

What You Do	How You Do It

Computer Needing Help:

1. At the computer needing help, **configure the computer to support Remote Desktop connections.**

a. **Open the System Properties dialog box.**

b. **Click the Remote tab.**

c. **Check the Allow Users To Connect Remotely To This Computer check box.**

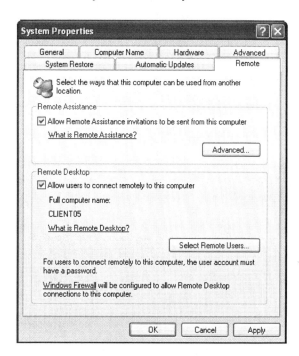

 You're going to connect to your partner's computer as Administrator, so you don't have to grant permissions to a user account to use Remote Desktop by clicking Select Remote Users.

d. **Click OK.**

Helper Computer:

2. At the helper computer, **connect to the other computer using Remote Desktop Connection.**

    a. On your computer, **choose Start→All Programs→Accessories→ Communications→Remote Desktop Connection.**

    b. In the Computer text box, **type** *the name of your partner's computer*

    c. **Click Connect.**

    d. **Log on as** *Administrator* **with a password of** *!Pass1234* **and press Enter.**

    e. **Verify that you can see the other computer's desktop.**

 When you make the connection, your partner will see the logon screen.

    f. **Log off from your remote session with your partner's computer.**

    g. If time permits, **reverse roles and repeat the activity.**

Check Your Knowledge

1. What is the purpose of Remote Desktop?

_____

_____

2. Can anyone access another computer using Remote Desktop?

_____

_____

EXERCISE 9-6

Restoring System State Data

Setup:

You have backed up the System State data for Windows XP to C:\Backup\Backup.bkf.

Scenario:

A programmer just installed a custom application he developed on one of your client's computers. The client has contacted you because he's now experiencing problems with his computer. You aren't sure what the custom application changed on the computer. Fortunately, you scheduled a System State data backup to take place on a regular basis; the last backup occurred last night.

 There is a simulated version of this activity available on the CD-ROM that shipped with this course. You can run this simulation on any Windows computer to review the activity after class, or as an alternative to performing the activity as a group in class. The activity simulation can be launched either directly from the CD-ROM by clicking the Interactives link and navigating to the appropriate one, or from the installed data file location by opening the C:\085820Data\Simulations\Lesson#\Activity# folder and double-clicking the executable (.exe) file.

What You Do	How You Do It
1. **Restore the System State data.**	a. **Open Backup.**
	b. **Click Next.**
	c. **Select Restore Files And Settings and then click Next.**
	d. **Expand the media set and check the System State check box.**
	e. **Click Next.**
	f. **Click Advanced.**
	g. On the Where To Restore page, to accept the default of Original Location, **click Next and then click OK.**
	h. On the How To Restore page, **select Replace Existing Files and click Next.**
	i. On the Advanced Restore Options page, **click Next.**
	j. To start the restoration process, **click Finish.**
	k. When the restore is complete, **click Close.**
	l. When prompted, to restart the computer, **click Yes.**
	m. The restart might take longer than normal. When it completes, **log back on to the computer.**

Check Your Knowledge

1. When restoring a System State data backup set, what two options must be set for the restore operation to be successful?

2. After restoring the system, it seems rebooting takes much longer than normal. Is the computer still having issues?

_____

_____

_____

_____

EXERCISE 9-7

Restoring the System to a Restore Point

Setup:

In this activity, you will create a restore point and restore the system to that restore point.

Scenario:

One of your hardware suppliers has just posted some updated device drivers to their website, and they recommend that all their clients install these drivers. However, none of the drivers are signed. You know that you could roll back a single driver if you have problems with it, but in this case, you have several different files to update. You're not sure exactly what the ramifications to the system will be. Before you start installing the new drivers, you would like to be sure that you have a way to bring the system back to its current state if you encounter problems. You decide to use a restore point; because you have not created a manual restore point before, you want to test the restore point after you create it.

 There is a simulated version of this activity available on the CD-ROM that shipped with this course. You can run this simulation on any Windows computer to review the activity after class, or as an alternative to performing the activity as a group in class. The activity simulation can be launched either directly from the CD-ROM by clicking the Interactives link and navigating to the appropriate one, or from the installed data file location by opening the C:\085820Data\Simulations\Lesson#\Activity# folder and double-clicking the executable (.exe) file.

What You Do	**How You Do It**
1. Configure a manual restore point.	a. Choose Start→All Programs→ Accessories→System Tools→System Restore.
	b. Select Create A Restore Point. Click Next.
	To begin, select the task that you want to perform:
	○ Restore my computer to an earlier time
	⦿ Create a restore point
	c. In the Restore Point Description text box, **type *New Drivers***
	d. Click Create.

2. **Verify the restore point by restoring the system.**

a. **Click Home.**

b. **Select Restore My Computer To An Earlier Time. Click Next.**

c. Dates listed in bold contain restore points. **Verify that the New Drivers restore point is selected in the list for the current day. Click Next.**

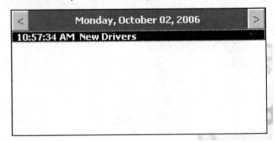

d. **Read the Confirm Restore Point Selection information and click Next.**

e. The system shuts down and restarts, and files are restored from the restore point. When the system has restarted, to log on, enter *!Pass1234*

f. To close System Restore, **click OK.**

Check Your Knowledge

1. What are system restore points?

_____

_____

2. How can you restore a system to an earlier restore point?

_____

_____

_____

EXERCISE 9-8

Recovering the System With Last Known Good

Objective:

In this activity, you will create a boot problem with the keyboard, and then correct the problem by using Last Known Good.

Scenario:

A change to the configuration of the keyboard driver is completely preventing user logons. Because the keyboard is not responding, even the Administrator can't log on to fix the problem. You need to restore system functionality so that users can log on again.

 There is a simulated version of this activity available on the CD-ROM that shipped with this course. You can run this simulation on any Windows computer to review the activity after class, or as an alternative to performing the activity as a group in class. The activity simulation can be launched either directly from the CD-ROM by clicking the Interactives link and navigating to the appropriate one, or from the installed data file location by opening the C:\ 085820Data\Simulations\Lesson#\Activity# folder and double-clicking the executable (.exe) file.

What You Do	How You Do It
1. **Modify the Registry to prevent the Kbdclass device from loading.**	a. To run Registry Editor, **Choose Start→ Run, type *regedit* and click OK.**
	b. In Registry Editor, **expand HKEY_ LOCAL_MACHINE\System\ CurrentControlSet\Services.**
	c. **Scroll down and select the Kbdclass subkey.**
	d. **Double-click the Start value entry.**

e. A Start value of 4 will prevent the driver from loading, which simulates a corrupt keyboard driver. In the Value Data text box, **type *4* and click OK.**

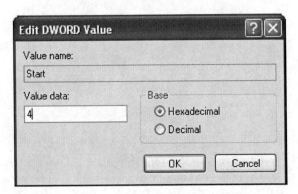

f. **Close Registry Editor.**

2. **Test the keyboard problem.**

a. **Choose Start→Turn Off Computer. Click Restart.**

b. The computer boots and the Welcome Screen appears. **Attempt to type your password. You will be unable to do so.**

3. **Why are you unable to log on?**

4. **Why won't Safe Mode work in this situation?**

a) Because the keyboard is one of the Safe Mode devices. If you disable the driver, the keyboard won't work even in Safe Mode.

b) Because you have already logged on.

c) Because Safe Mode is not a troubleshooting tool.

d) Because you have not configured a Restore Point.

5. **Use the Last Known Good configuration to start the computer.**

    a. **Use the power button to turn the computer off and on again.**

    b. After the POST sequence and before the progress bar, **press F8.**

    c. **Select Last Known Good Configuration, and then press Enter.**

    d. **Verify that Microsoft Windows XP Professional is selected and press Enter.**

    e. **Enter your password to log on.**

Check Your Knowledge

1. What does restoring the system with the Last Known Good option do?

EXERCISE 9-9

Testing the Recovery Console

Setup:
You have the Windows XP Professional installation CD-ROM available.

Scenario:
You are spending your day visiting the desktops of a number of users who have reported severe system problems. Not all the systems have Recovery Console installed as a boot option, so you have a copy of the Windows XP Professional CD-ROM available. Once you boot to Recovery Console, however, you need to select the appropriate tools and techniques to correct the specific problem for each system.

There is a simulated version of this activity available on the CD-ROM that shipped with this course. You can run this simulation on any Windows computer to review the activity after class, or as an alternative to performing the activity as a group in class. The activity simulation can be launched either directly from the CD-ROM by clicking the Interactives link and navigating to the appropriate one, or from the installed data file location by opening the C:\085820Data\Simulations\Lesson#\Activity# folder and double-clicking the executable (.exe) file.

What You Do	How You Do It
1. Use Recovery Console to start the computer.	a. **Insert the Windows XP Professional CD-ROM.**
	b. **Choose Start→Turn Off Computer and click Restart.**
	c. When prompted, **press any key to boot from the CD-ROM.**
	d. On the Welcome To Setup screen, to boot to Recovery Console, **press R.**
	e. At the Which Windows Installation Would You Like To Log On To prompt, **enter 1**
	f. If you reinstalled Windows XP Professional earlier in this course, the Administrator password is blank. To log on, **press Enter.**
	If you did not reinstall Windows XP Professional, the Administrator password is !Pass1234. To log on, type **!Pass1234 and press Enter.**
2. View Help system entries on various Recovery Console commands.	a. At the C:\Windows prompt, to display a list of supported Recovery Console commands, **enter help**
	b. **Press the Spacebar key to scroll to the end of the list.**
	c. To view the Help information on the bootcfg command, **enter help bootcfg**
	d. **View Help information on other Recovery Console commands of your choice.**
	e. To exit Recovery Console and restart the computer, **enter exit**
	f. **Enter your password to log on.**
	g. **Remove the installation CD-ROM.**

3. **Use the Help information to match the system problem with the most likely method for correcting it in Recovery Console.**

⎯	After performing some disk management tasks, a user has been unable to restart his computer. The user sees an Unreadable Boot Disk message.	a.	Use the enable command to enable the service.
⎯	A user has manually disabled a key startup service.	b.	Use the delete command to delete pagefile.sys. The file will be re-created at the next startup.
⎯	A user installed a new, unsigned driver and the system will not start.	c.	Use Fixmbr, which rewrites the MBR, or Fixboot, which rewrites the boot sector of the system volume.
⎯	A user deleted the Ntdetect.com file.	d.	Use the expand and copy commands to copy a new version of the file from the Windows XP Professional installation media.
⎯	The Windows pagefile has become corrupt.	e.	Use the disable command to disable the driver. When you reboot, you can remove the driver.
⎯	NTLDR will not load.	f.	Use the bootcfg command.

Check Your Knowledge

1. What is Recovery Console?

_____

_____

2. When using Recovery Console, how can you resolve an NTLDR failing to load?

_____

_____

3. When using Recovery Console, how can you reconfigure boot devices?

_____

4. Can you run Recovery Console from the hard drive?

_____

_____

_____

EXERCISE 9-10

Creating and Testing a Windows XP Boot Floppy Disk

Setup:

You will need a blank floppy disk for this activity. Your computer system BIOS is configured to boot from the floppy drive.

Scenario:

You're updating your troubleshooting toolkit, and you realize that you don't have a boot floppy disk for the new Windows XP Professional installations in your company. You decide to use your desktop computer to create a Windows XP Professional boot floppy disk.

There is a simulated version of this activity available on the CD-ROM that shipped with this course. You can run this simulation on any Windows computer to review the activity after class, or as an alternative to performing the activity as a group in class. The activity simulation can be launched either directly from the CD-ROM by clicking the Interactives link and navigating to the appropriate one, or from the installed data file location by opening the C:\ 085820Data\Simulations\Lesson#\Activity# folder and double-clicking the executable (.exe) file.

What You Do	How You Do It
1. Format a floppy disk.	a. **Place a blank floppy disk in your computer's floppy-disk drive.**
	b. **Open My Computer.**
	c. **Right-click the floppy drive icon and choose Format.**
	d. **Check Quick Format and click Start.**

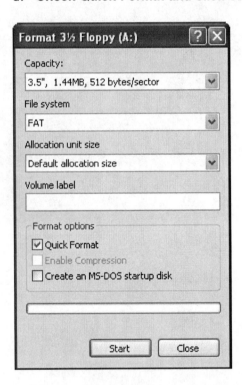

e. To confirm the format, **click OK.**

f. When the format is complete, **click OK.**

g. **Click Close.**

2. Configure Windows Explorer options to show protected operating system files.

a. In My Computer, **open the C drive.**

b. **If necessary, click Show The Contents Of This Folder.**

c. **Choose Tools→Folder Options.**

d. **Click the View tab.**

e. **If necessary, select Show Hidden Files And Folders.**

f. **If necessary, uncheck Hide Extensions For Known File Types.**

g. **Uncheck Hide Protected Operating System Files (Recommended).**

h. To confirm the change, **click Yes.**

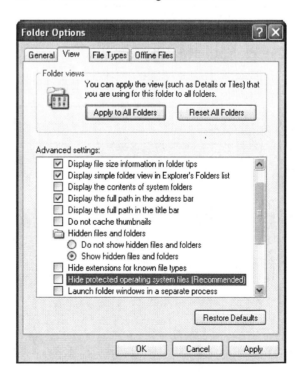

i. **Click OK.**

		j.	Verify that you can now see the system files.
3.	Copy the required files to the boot floppy disk.	a.	In the C:\ folder, **select the Boot.ini, Ntldr, and Ntdetect.com files.**
		b.	**If you have a Bootsect.dos file or an Ntbootdd.sys file, select those files as well.**
		c.	**Right-click any selected file and choose Send To→3 1/2 Floppy (A).**
		d.	**Close the window.**
4.	Test the boot floppy disk.	a.	**Choose Start→Turn Off Computer and click Restart.**
		b.	The system will locate the disk in the floppy drive and boot from that drive instead of the C drive. **Enter your password to log on.**
		c.	**Remove the floppy disk from the drive and label it.**

Check Your Knowledge

1. Can Windows XP be booted from a floppy disk?

_____

_____

_____

_____

LAB 9-1

Preparing for Automated System Recovery (ASR)

Activity Time: 20 minutes

Scenario:

 You can find a suggested solution for this activity in the \Solutions\PreparingforASR.txt file in the data files location.

---

1. If you do not have a physical backup device, **create an empty 2 GB NTFS volume to store the ASR set.** Delete existing data partitions if necessary to create empty space.

---

2. **Create the ASR backup set.** This process can take several minutes.

---

3. **Create the ASR floppy disk.**

---

4. **Store the ASR disks in a safe location.**

10 | Network Technologies

Activities included in this chapter:

- Exercise 10-1 Identifying Network Concepts
- Exercise 10-2 Identifying the Local MAC Address
- Exercise 10-3 Identifying Local Network Media
- Exercise 10-4 Identifying Local Network Characteristics
- Exercise 10-5 Discussing Network Connectivity
- Exercise 10-6 Discussing Internet Technologies
- Lab 10-1 Selecting Network Technologies

EXERCISE 10-1

Identifying Network Concepts

Scenario:
In this activity, you will discuss basic network concepts and components.

1. **A group of computers connected together to communicate and share resources is known as:**

   a) A computer network.

   b) A server.

   c) A client.

   d) A workgroup.

2. **A network computer that shares resources with and responds to requests from other computers is known as a:**

   a) Client.

   b) Server.

   c) Terminal.

   d) Node.

3. **A network computer that utilizes the resources of other network computers is known as a:**

   a) Server.

   b) Host computer.

   c) Client.

   d) Node.

4. **A self-sufficient computer that both provides and uses resources is a:**

   a) Host computer.

   b) Client.

   c) Server.

   d) Peer.

5. **What is the best definition of a network model?**

   a) The physical layout of the network.

   b) A description of how the nodes on a network interact and share control of the network communications.

   c) Technical specifications for how to establish and maintain communications.

   d) The group of tools used for network administration and security.

6. **Match the network model with its description.**

   ___ Centralized network

   ___ Client/server network

   ___ Peer-to-peer network

   ___ Mixed mode network

   a. A network in which some nodes act as servers to provide special services on behalf of other nodes.

   b. A network in which resource sharing, processing, and communications control are completely decentralized.

   c. A network in which a central host computer controls all network communication and performs the data processing and storage on behalf of network clients.

   d. A network that displays characteristics of more than one of the three standard network models.

7. **You cannot log on to the network. You check the back of your network adapter and see one steady light and one flickering light. What does this tell you?**

   a) That there is a network connection, but the system is not receiving data.

   b) That there is no network connection.

   c) That there is a network connection and the system is receiving data.

   d) That the network adapter has a defect.

8. **Match the media type with its definition.**

   ___ IEEE 1394

   ___ Fiber optic

   ___ Twisted pair

   ___ Coaxial

   a. Multiple insulated conductors clad in a protective and insulating outer jacket carry the signal. Wires are grouped in colored pairs.

   b. A shielded cable, similar to STP, with either four or six conductors that can be used to connect up to 63 devices to form a small local network.

   c. The least sensitive of any cable type; light pulses from a laser or high-intensity LED carry the signal through the core.

   d. A central copper conductor carries the signal. It is surrounded by braided or foil shielding designed to reduce electromagnetic interference. A dialectic insulator separates the conductor from the shield.

9. **Identify the type of network cabling shown in the illustration.**

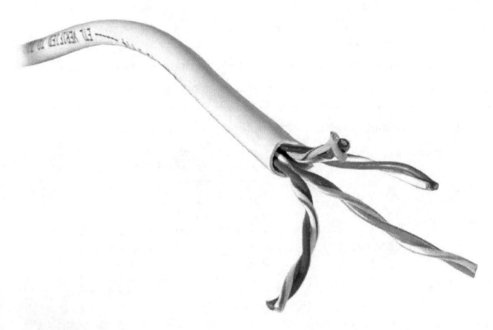

a) Twisted pair

b) Coax

c) Fiber optic

10. **Identify the type of network cabling shown in the illustration.**

a) Unshielded twisted pair

b) Shielded twisted pair

c) Coax

d) Fiber optic

11. **Select the reason or reasons that plenum cable is permitted in air handling spaces and can be run through firebreaks.**

    a) It does not give off noxious or poisonous gases when burned.

    b) It gives off noxious or poisonous gases when burned.

    c) Fire cannot travel through the cable because the jacket is closely formed to the conductors.

    d) Fire can travel through the cable because the jacket loosely surrounds the conductors.

    e) It is stiffer than PVC cable.

Check Your Knowledge

1. What is the primary difference between a computer network and a workgroup?

2. How is a peer-to-peer network different from a client/server network?

3. What is a mixed mode network?

4. How can you easily verify that there is connectivity between your computer and the rest of the network?

5. What is the difference between Plenum and PVC cable?

EXERCISE 10-2

Identifying the Local MAC Address

Scenario:
In this activity, you will identify your computer's MAC address.

 There is a simulated version of this activity available on the CD-ROM that shipped with this course. You can run this simulation on any Windows computer to review the activity after class, or as an alternative to performing the activity as a group in class. The activity simulation can be launched either directly from the CD-ROM by clicking the Interactives link and navigating to the appropriate one, or from the installed data file location by opening the C:\085820Data\Simulations\Lesson#\Activity# folder and double-clicking the executable (.exe) file.

What You Do	How You Do It
1. **Open the Status dialog box for your Local Area Connection.**	a. **Choose Start→Control Panel.**
	b. **Click Network And Internet Connections.**
	c. **Click Network Connections.**
	d. **Right-click Local Area Connection and choose Status.**

2. **Identify your MAC address.**

   a. **Click the Support tab.**

   b. **Click Details.**

   c. To determine the MAC address, **identify the Physical Address value.**

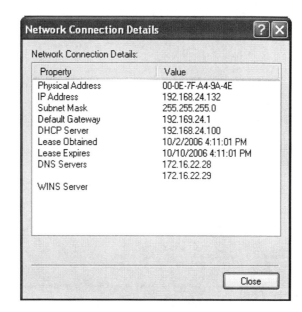

   d. **Click Close twice.**

 You can leave the Network Connections window open.

Check Your Knowledge

1. What is a MAC address, and how does it differ from an IP address?

_____

_____

2. In addition to examining the network adapter, how else can you obtain a network adapter's MAC address?

_____

_____

EXERCISE 10-3

Identifying Local Network Media

Scenario:
In this activity, you will identify the network media used on your local classroom network.

---

1. **Identify the cable type used to connect your computer to the classroom network.**

---

2. **Identify the types of connectors used in the classroom network.**

---

3. **Your instructor might provide samples of a variety of media and connector types. Identify each of the media and connectors.**

Check Your Knowledge

1. What is the most prevalent type of network cable used to connect computers to a network?

---

2. What is an RJ-45 connector?

EXERCISE 10-4

Identifying Local Network Characteristics

Scenario:

In this activity, you will identify your computer's network protocol, address, and name.

 There is a simulated version of this activity available on the CD-ROM that shipped with this course. You can run this simulation on any Windows computer to review the activity after class, or as an alternative to performing the activity as a group in class. The activity simulation can be launched either directly from the CD-ROM by clicking the Interactives link and navigating to the appropriate one, or from the installed data file location by opening the C:\ 085820Data\Simulations\Lesson#\Activity# folder and double-clicking the executable (.exe) file.

What You Do	How You Do It
1. **Determine the protocol in use on your system.**	a. In the Network Connections window, **right-click Local Area Connection and choose Properties.**
	b. In the This Connection Uses The Following Items box, **verify that Internet Protocol (TCP/IP) is listed.**

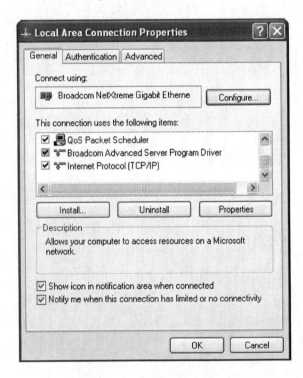

	c. To close the Properties dialog box, **click OK.**
2. **View the TCP/IP information assigned to your network card.**	a. **Right-click Local Area Connection and choose Status.**
	b. **Click the Support tab.**

c. In the Connection Status section, **view the IP address, subnet mask, and default gateway information.**

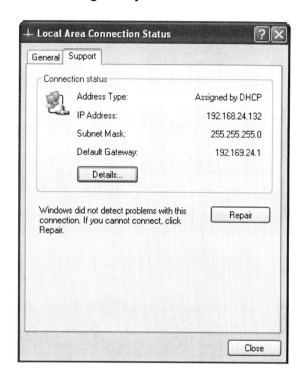

d. **Click Close.**

3. Determine your network name.

    a. In the Network Connections window, under Other Places, **click My Computer.**

    b. Under System Tasks, **click View System Information.**

    c. In the System Properties dialog box, **click the Computer Name tab.**

    d. On Windows systems, the host name is the same as the computer name assigned at installation. **Determine the Full Computer Name and click OK.**

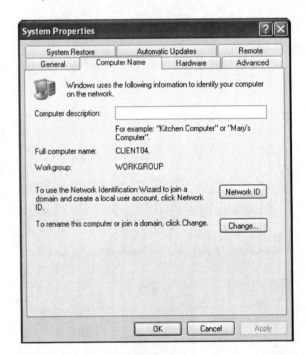

    e. **Click My Network Places.**

    f. To return to the Network Connections window, **click View Network Connections.**

4. Match each component of a TCP/IP network implementation with its description.

___ Host portion of address	a. Separates host and network addresses to determine if communications are local and remote
___ Network portion of address	b. Identifies a logical or physical segment of the network
___ Subnet mask	c. Provides a path for communications to leave the local network and reach remote hosts
___ Default gateway	d. Identifies an individual TCP/IP node

5. **Match the IP address class with its use.**

___	Class A	a.	Multicast addresses
___	Class B	b.	A large number of networks with a large number of hosts each
___	Class C	c.	Many networks with few hosts each
___	Class D	d.	Experimentation and research
___	Class E	e.	Few networks with many hosts each

6. **Where would you most likely find the IPX/SPX protocol?**

    a) On an older Novell NetWare network.

    b) On the Internet.

    c) On a small Windows XP-based home network.

    d) On an old Windows for Workgroups network.

Check Your Knowledge

1. How can you determine the protocol being used by your computer's network connection?

    _____

    _____

2. What is the most common protocol used for network connectivity?

    _____

3. What is the function of a TCP/IP network's subnet mask?

    _____

4. What function does specifying the default gateway serve?

    _____

    _____

5. How many different IP address classes are there and what are their specified uses?

    _____

    _____

    _____

    _____

    _____

EXERCISE 10-5

Discussing Network Connectivity

Scenario:
In this activity, you will discuss network connectivity technologies.

1. The company Chester Unlimited has a remote office that must have access to its corporate office with relatively high bandwidth. This network fits the category of a:

   a) LAN.

   b) WAN.

   c) CAN.

   d) GAN.

2. Williams Ltd. occupies four floors in the East building of the River View Business Complex. Their network would fit the category of a:

   a) LAN.

   b) WAN.

   c) CAN.

   d) GAN.

3. The transmission method that allows multiple signals to be carried separately on the same media at the same time is:

   a) Baseband.

   b) Broadband.

   c) Modulated.

   d) Multicast.

4. Match the broadband communications method to its description.

   ___ DSL

   ___ Cable modem

   ___ Satellite

   ___ ISDN

   a. Not technically broadband, it transmits voice and data over phone lines and has basic rate and primary rate services.

   b. Transmits digital signals over existing telephone lines.

   c. Transmits over extremely long distances.

   d. A high-speed way to transmit both data and TV signals on the same physical media.

5. **Match the wireless technology with its description.**

___	Cellular WAN	a.	Provides broadband Internet coverage in rural or remote areas.
___	Satellite	b.	A popular standards-based wireless radio network implementation.
___	WiFi	c.	A short-range radio technology often used for communications between personal digital devices.
___	Infrared	d.	A generally short-range wireless connection method requiring direct line of sight.
___	Bluetooth	e.	Transmits network data over mobile phone technologies.

6. **Which of the following are wired connection technologies?**

   a) Bluetooth

   b) ISDN

   c) Dial-up connections

   d) WiFi

7. **Which are wireless connection technologies?**

   a) Bluetooth

   b) Fiber optic

   c) 802.11

   d) Cellular WAN

   e) Twisted-pair

Check Your Knowledge

1. What is the purpose of a wide area network?

   _____

   _____

2. What is broadband?

   _____

   _____

3. Identify the more common wireless technologies.

   _____

   _____

EXERCISE 10-6

Discussing Internet Technologies

Scenario:

In this activity, you will discuss Internet technologies.

1. **Match the protocol with its definition.**

   ___ SMTP

   ___ IMAP

   ___ HTML

   ___ HTTP

   a. The authoring language used to create documents on the web.

   b. A communications protocol used to retrieve messages from an email server.

   c. The communication protocol that downloads web page files from the web server to the client browser.

   d. A communications protocol used to send email to a mail server.

2. **SSL is a security protocol that uses certificates for _____ ___ _____ to protect web communication.**

3. **How do SSL-enabled URLs begin?**

   a) shttp://

   b) http://

   c) https://

   d) hssl://

4. **Telnet is:**

   a) A terminal emulation protocol that enables a user at one site to simulate a session on a remote host.

   b) Being rapidly adopted because it relies on the existing, robust router infrastructure of IP networks and the near-universal implementation of the IP protocol.

   c) A protocol used to upload files to or download files from an FTP file server.

   d) The most common protocol used to make web requests.

5. **VoIP is a voice over data implementation in which voice signals are transmitted over:**

   a) Telephone lines.

   b) IP networks.

   c) Cable networks.

   d) Infrared networks.

6. **What is the best protocol for transferring large amounts of file-based data over the Internet?**

   a) HTTP

   b) HTTPS

   c) IMAP4

   d) FTP

Check Your Knowledge

1. What are the protocols used in the transmission and reception of email messages?

   _____

2. What does a URL beginning with https:// indicate?

   _____

   _____

3. What is VoIP?

   _____

4. Which protocol is better to transmit large amounts of data over the Internet, IMAP or FTP?

   _____

   _____

LAB 10-1

Selecting Network Technologies

Activity Time: 20 minutes

Scenario:

---

1.   List the various networking technologies you would recommend for the Everything For Coffee branch office and explain how each technology would support the employees' connectivity needs. Are there any network components you will not employ? Are there any optional components? What are the pros and cons of implementing each one? You might wish to sketch a possible network design for this branch office to show the various connectivity components.

11 | Installing and Managing Network Connections

Activities included in this chapter:

- Exercise 11-1 Configuring TCP/IP Manually
- Exercise 11-2 Configuring TCP/IP Automatically
- Exercise 11-3 Installing the NetWare Client
- Exercise 11-4 Removing the NetWare Client
- Exercise 11-5 Configuring a Web Browser on a Windows XP Computer
- Exercise 11-6 Troubleshooting TCP/IP Problems
- Lab 11-1 Troubleshooting a Network Connection

EXERCISE 11-1

Configuring TCP/IP Manually

Setup:

Use an IP address of 192.168.200.#, where # is your computer number. The subnet mask is 255.255.255.0. The preferred DNS server's address is 192.168.200.200.

Scenario:

As an A+ technician, you receive a support call from a client stating that her new Windows XP Professional laptop can't connect to her office's small network. When you review the computer's configuration, you determine that it's attempting to obtain an IP address from a DHCP server. Your client's network doesn't have a DHCP server. Instead, all computers are configured manually with IP addresses.

 There is a simulated version of this activity available on the CD-ROM that shipped with this course. You can run this simulation on any Windows computer to review the activity after class, or as an alternative to performing the activity as a group in class. The activity simulation can be launched either directly from the CD-ROM by clicking the Interactives link and navigating to the appropriate one, or from the installed data file location by opening the C:\085820Data\Simulations\Lesson#\Activity# folder and double-clicking the executable (.exe) file.

What You Do	How You Do It
1. Configure the TCP/IP protocol.	a. In the Network Connections window, **right-click the Local Area Connection and choose Properties.**

b.   In the list of network components, **select Internet Protocol (TCP/IP).**

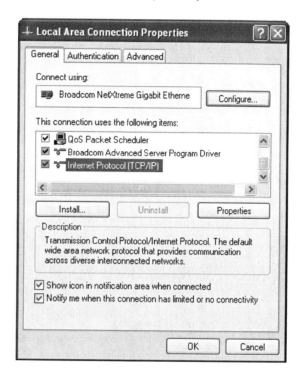

c.   **Click Properties.**

d.   **Select Use The Following IP Address.**

e.   In the IP Address text box, **type *192.168. 200.#*,** where *#* is your assigned computer number.

f.   **Press Tab.**

g.   In the Subnet Mask text box, **verify that the subnet mask is 255.255.255.0.**

h. In the Preferred DNS Server text box,
type *192.168.200.200*

Internet Protocol (TCP/IP) Properties

General

You can get IP settings assigned automatically if your network supports
this capability. Otherwise, you need to ask your network administrator for
the appropriate IP settings.

○ Obtain an IP address automatically

◉ Use the following IP address:

IP address:	192 . 168 . 200 . 4
Subnet mask:	255 . 255 . 255 . 0
Default gateway:	. . .

○ Obtain DNS server address automatically

◉ Use the following DNS server addresses:

Preferred DNS server:	192 . 168 . 200 . 200
Alternate DNS server:	. . .

Advanced...

OK   Cancel

i. **Click OK, then click Close.**

2. **Verify the IP addressing
configuration.**

a. **Choose Start→All Programs→
Accessories→Command Prompt.**

b. **Enter `ipconfig /all`**

c. **Verify that the IP address, subnet
mask, and DNS server address information for the Local Area Connection
are correct.**

3. **Test TCP/IP connectivity.**

    a. To verify that you can communicate on the network using the TCP/IP protocol, in the Command Prompt window, **type ping 192.168.200.100**

    b. **Verify that you receive four successful replies. Close the Command Prompt window.**

Check Your Knowledge

1. Why would you have to manually configure a computer's IP address?

2. Which parameters must you enter when manually configuring an IP address?

EXERCISE 11-2

Configuring TCP/IP Automatically

Scenario:

One of your clients, a growing company, has just implemented DHCP servers to reduce the administrative workload for assigning IP addresses. The network administrator has configured the DHCP server to provide computers with an appropriate IP address, subnet mask, and DNS server address. As an A+ technician, you've been called in to assist with configuring the client's Windows XP computers to use DHCP.

 There is a simulated version of this activity available on the CD-ROM that shipped with this course. You can run this simulation on any Windows computer to review the activity after class, or as an alternative to performing the activity as a group in class. The activity simulation can be launched either directly from the CD-ROM by clicking the Interactives link and navigating to the appropriate one, or from the installed data file location by opening the C:\085820Data\Simulations\Lesson#\Activity# folder and double-clicking the executable (.exe) file.

What You Do	How You Do It
1. **Configure your computer to obtain its IP address and DNS server address information automatically.**	a. In the Network Connections window, **display the properties of the Local Area Connection.**
	b. In the list of network components, **select Internet Protocol (TCP/IP).**
	c. **Click Properties.**
	d. **Select Obtain An IP Address Automatically.**
	e. **Select Obtain DNS Server Address Automatically.**
	f. **Click OK, and then click Close.**

2.	Verify and test the IP addressing configuration.	a.	Choose Start→Command Prompt.
		b.	Enter `ipconfig /all`
		c.	Verify that your computer has appropriate IP address information.
		d.	To test connectivity, **ping another class-room computer.**
		e.	**Close the Command Prompt window.**

Check Your Knowledge

1. What is the purpose of a DHCP server?

_____

_____

EXERCISE 11-3

Installing the NetWare Client

Scenario:

One of your clients has discovered that she needs to retrieve some data from a legacy NetWare server before she decommissions the server. She has asked you to add the necessary network connectivity components to her Windows XP system. Once the NetWare client support is installed, she can configure the logon information she needs to access the server.

 There is a simulated version of this activity available on the CD-ROM that shipped with this course. You can run this simulation on any Windows computer to review the activity after class, or as an alternative to performing the activity as a group in class. The activity simulation can be launched either directly from the CD-ROM by clicking the Interactives link and navigating to the appropriate one, or from the installed data file location by opening the C:\ 085820Data\Simulations\Lesson#\Activity# folder and double-clicking the executable (.exe) file.

What You Do	How You Do It
1. **Install Client Service For NetWare.**	a. **Open the properties for the Local Area Connection.** b. **Click Install.** c. **Verify that Client is selected and click Add.** d. **Select Client Service For NetWare and click OK.**

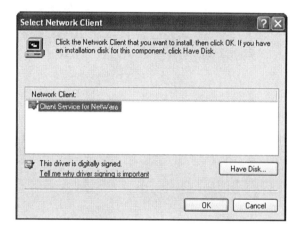

e. **Click Yes** to restart the computer.

f. **Log back on to the computer as Admin#.**

 Installing CSNW automatically reconfigures Windows to use the Log On To Windows dialog box instead of the Welcome screen.

g. In the Select NetWare Logon dialog box, **verify that <None> is selected in the Preferred Server drop-down list, and then click OK.**

h. **Click OK** to close the Select NetWare Logon dialog box.

2. **Verify the installed network components.**

   a. **Display the properties for the Local Area Connection.**

   b. In the This Connection Uses The Following Items list, **verify that Client Service For NetWare appears along with Client For Microsoft Networks.**

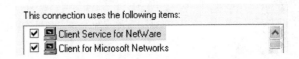

   c. **Scroll the list and verify that NWLink NetBIOS and NWLink IPX/SPX/NetBIOS Compatible Transport Protocol appear as installed protocols.**

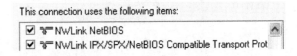

   d. **Close the Local Area Connection Properties.**

   e. **Click the Back button twice.**

3. View the network client properties.

a. In the Control Panel task pane, **click Other Control Panel Options.**

b. **Click CSNW.**

c. You could use this tool to configure a different server or tree and context, as well as print and logon script options. **Click Cancel.**

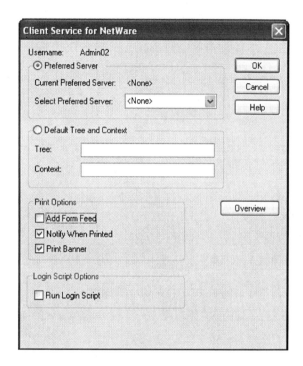

Check Your Knowledge

1. Is it possible to connect a Windows XP machine to a Novell network?

2. Which protocols are used when connecting a Windows XP machine to a Novell network?

EXERCISE 11-4

Removing the NetWare Client

Scenario:

Your client has obtained the data she needed from the NetWare server and has decommissioned the servers. She has asked you to remove the NetWare client components from her Windows XP system.

 There is a simulated version of this activity available on the CD-ROM that shipped with this course. You can run this simulation on any Windows computer to review the activity after class, or as an alternative to performing the activity as a group in class. The activity simulation can be launched either directly from the CD-ROM by clicking the Interactives link and navigating to the appropriate one, or from the installed data file location by opening the C:\ 085820Data\Simulations\Lesson#\Activity# folder and double-clicking the executable (.exe) file.

What You Do	How You Do It
1. **Remove NetWare Client and NWLink IPX/SPX protocol.**	a. **Display the properties for the Local Area Connection.**
	b. **Select Client Service For NetWare and click Uninstall.**
	c. **Click Yes** to confirm that you want to uninstall Client Service For NetWare.
	d. **Click Yes** to restart the computer.
	e. When prompted, **log on as Admin#.**
	f. **Verify that the NWLink IPX/SPX protocol has been removed.**

EXERCISE 11-5

Configuring a Web Browser on a Windows XP Computer

Setup:

This activity requires Internet connectivity. If necessary, before you start this activity, configure your network settings so you can connect to the Internet.

Scenario:

The management at EverythingForCoffee.com has recently realized that the value of allowing their employees to access critical business information located on the Internet outweighs the risks of personal web browsing on company time. They have hired you to configure all their Windows XP computers for Internet access on their company LAN.

There is a simulated version of this activity available on the CD-ROM that shipped with this course. You can run this simulation on any Windows computer to review the activity after class, or as an alternative to performing the activity as a group in class. The activity simulation can be launched either directly from the CD-ROM by clicking the Interactives link and navigating to the appropriate one, or from the installed data file location by opening the C:\ 085820Data\Simulations\Lesson#\Activity# folder and double-clicking the executable (.exe) file.

What You Do	How You Do It
1. **Set up an Internet connection on your computer.**	a. **Choose Start→Control Panel.**
	b. **Click Network And Internet Connections.**
	c. **Click Network Connections.**
	d. At the left of the screen, under Network Tasks, **click Create A New Connection.**
	e. **Click Next.**
	f. On the Network Connection Type page, if necessary, **select Connect To The Internet.**
	g. With Connect To The Internet selected on the Network Connection Type page, **click Next.**
	h. On the Getting Ready page, **select Set Up My Connection Manually.**
	i. **Click Next.**
	j. On the Internet Connection page, **select Connect Using A Broadband Connection That Is Always On.**
	k. **Click Next.**
	l. **Click Finish.**
	m. **Close the Network Connections window.**

2.	Set the home page of Internet Explorer to Everything For Coffee.com.	a.	**Choose Start→Internet.**
		b.	In Internet Explorer, **choose Tools→ Internet Options.**
		c.	In the Home Page region, in the Address field, **type** *http://www. everythingforcoffee.com*
		d.	**Click OK.**
		e.	To test the new home page, **click the Home button.**
		f.	**Close Internet Explorer.**

Check Your Knowledge

1. Why is it necessary to configure an Internet connection for a computer in which Windows XP Professional was just installed?

_____

_____

_____

2. Where can you adjust Internet Explorer's options and customize its features?

_____

EXERCISE 11-6

Troubleshooting TCP/IP Problems

Scenario:

Your company provides technical support to a number of different clients. These clients have networks that range in size from only a few computers to as many as hundreds of computers. As an A+ technician, your job is to troubleshoot connectivity problems that your clients report.

1. One of your clients calls to report that he is unable to connect to any network resources or the Internet. After questioning him, you've determined that someone accidentally unplugged the DHCP server. The client reports that the DHCP server is up and running, but he's still unable to connect to any resources. You have the client type in ipconfig /all and he reports the following results:

   • IP address: 169.254.225.48

   • Subnet mask: 255.255.0.0

   • Default gateway: None

   • DNS server: None

   After reviewing your company's documentation for this client's network, you've determined that the client's IP address should be on the 192.168.200.# network with a subnet mask of 255.255.255.0. The default gateway address is 192.168.200.1.

   What should you try next to attempt to solve the problem?

   a) Have the client open a command prompt window and enter ping 127.0.0.1.

   b) Have the client open a command prompt window and enter ping 192.168.200.1.

   c) Have the client open a command prompt window and enter ipconfig /release and ipconfig /renew.

   d) Have the client manually configure his IP address to one on the 192.168.200.# network, a subnet mask of 255.255.255.0, and a default gateway address of 192.168. 200.1.

2. **You receive a call from a client who reports that she's unable to access any websites in Internet Explorer. While talking with this user, you verify that she can ping the server's IP address on her network segment, the IP address of the default gateway, and the IP address of a computer on another network segment. You also determine that none of the other users on her network can connect to websites in Internet Explorer.**

   What might be the problem?

   a) Her network's default gateway server is down.

   b) Her network's DNS server is down.

   c) Her computer is configured with the wrong default gateway address.

   d) Her computer is configured with the wrong subnet mask.

3. **One of your clients reports that he is unable to see computers when he opens My Network Places.**

   Which step should you take first?

   a) Ask the client to ping another computer on his network.

   b) Determine if any of the other users on the network are experiencing problems.

   c) Ask the client to verify that the DHCP server is running.

   d) Ask the client to run ipconfig /release and ipconfig /renew.

4. **A client reports that he's unable to connect to any computers on the network or the Internet. You have him run the ipconfig command, and all his TCP/IP addressing parameters are correct. When you have him ping other computers on the network, his computer is unable to reach them. This computer is the only one that's experiencing a problem.**

   What should you check next?

   a) That his computer's network cable is plugged in to both the network card and the wall jack.

   b) That the DNS server is on and functioning properly.

   c) That the default gateway is on and functioning properly.

   d) That the DHCP server is on and functioning properly.

5. **Your client tells you that she has just installed a new server on her network. This server has a CD-ROM tower in it that she wants to share with all users on the network. No users can connect to this computer. All of her users can connect to other resources on the network and the Internet.**

   Which configuration parameter might be the cause of this problem?

   a) The server's IP address

   b) The users' IP addresses

   c) The users' subnet masks

   d) The server's default gateway

Check Your Knowledge

1. When examining a computer's connectivity to the network, what does an IP address that begins with 169.*.*.* indicate?

   _____

   _____

   _____

   _____

   _____

2. What is indicated by a computer's inability to access websites even though it can access sites by IP address?

   _____

   _____

3. What should you see when you access My Network Places on a networked computer?

   _____

   _____

LAB 11-1

Troubleshooting a Network Connection

Activity Time: 15 minutes

Scenario:

 You can find a suggested solution for this activity in the \Solutions\Troubleshooting a Network Connection.txt file in the data file location.

---

1. Examine the network connection settings to identify any problems.

---

2. Examine the local system's network connection hardware and cabling to identify any problems.

---

3. Use the Help And Support Center to troubleshoot the network connection.

---

4. Correct any problems you find during your investigation.

---

5. Test to verify the problem has been corrected.

---

6. Document the problem, your diagnostic steps, and the solution.

12 | Supporting Laptops and Portable Computing Devices

Activities included in this chapter:

- Exercise 12-1 Identifying Portable Computing Components
- Exercise 12-2 Configuring Power Management for Mobile Computing
- Exercise 12-3 Exchanging Portable Computer Drives
- Exercise 12-4 Docking Portable Systems
- Exercise 12-5 Installing PC Cards
- Exercise 12-6 Exchanging PC Cards
- Exercise 12-7 Installing a Mini-PCI Card
- Exercise 12-8 Adding Memory to Portable Computing Devices
- Exercise 12-9 Connecting Infrared Devices
- Exercise 12-10 Connecting Bluetooth Devices
- Exercise 12-11 Discussing Laptop and Portable Computing Device Troubleshooting
- Lab 12-1 Supporting Portable Computing Devices

EXERCISE 12-1

Identifying Portable Computing Components

Scenario:
In this activity, you will identify portable computing components.

1. **Which of the following are input devices commonly found on portable computing devices?**

   a) Numeric keypad

   b) Touch screen

   c) Trackpoint

   d) Function keys

   e) Full keyboards

2. **A laptop user needs to connect to a network wirelessly but does not have that functionality on his machine. What suggestions would you make to resolve this issue?**

   a) Upgrade the operating system.

   b) Purchase an Ethernet cable.

   c) Purchase a wireless PC card to insert in the machine's PCMCIA slot

   d) Purchase a USB wireless card.

3. **A user is looking to purchase a portable computing device for travel and wants your opinion on what device would best suit his needs. The user is looking for something to keep his appointments and contact names and numbers while on the road. Wireless E-mail access is also required. Which device would you suggest?**

   a) Laptop

   b) Sub-notebook

   c) PDA

   d) Tablet

Check Your Knowledge

1. What types of input devices can you find on portable computing devices such as PDAs?

   _____

   _____

   _____

2. How can you provide wireless connectivity to a device that lacks this functionality?

_____

_____

_____

3. What is the difference between a laptop and a PDA?

_____

_____

_____

_____

4. What is the purpose of a docking station with port replication?

_____

_____

_____

_____

_____

EXERCISE 12-2

Configuring Power Management for Mobile Computing

Scenario:

The department that you support has just received laptops running Windows XP Professional. Some users would like the power scheme changed so that when the laptops are running on battery power, the monitor turns itself off after 10 minutes and the hard disk turns itself off after 15 minutes. Computers should also be configured to modify the power management to support hibernation.

 There is a simulated version of this activity available on the CD-ROM that shipped with this course. You can run this simulation on any Windows computer to review the activity after class, or as an alternative to performing the activity as a group in class. The activity simulation can be launched either directly from the CD-ROM by clicking the Interactives link and navigating to the appropriate one, or from the installed data file location by opening the C:\085820Data\Simulations\Lesson#\Activity# folder and double-clicking the executable (.exe) file.

What You Do	**How You Do It**
1. **Create a custom power scheme.**	a. Choose **Start→Control Panel, and then click Performance And Maintenance.**
	b. **Click Power Options.**
	c. In the Power Options Properties dialog box, on the Advanced tab, **check Always Show Icon On The Taskbar.**
	d. On the Power Schemes tab, **click Save As.**
	e. In the Save Scheme dialog box, **type** *Mobile User* **and then click OK.**
	f. Under Settings For Mobile User Power Scheme, in the Running On Batteries column, **set Turn Off Monitor to After 10 Minutes.**
	g. In the Running On Batteries column, **set Turn Off Hard Disks to After 15 Minutes.**
	h. In the Power Options Properties dialog box, **click Apply.**
2. **Enable hibernation.**	a. In the Power Options Properties dialog box, on the Hibernate tab, **check Enable Hibernation.**
	b. **Click OK** to close the Power Options Properties dialog box, and then **close the Performance And Maintenance window.**

3. **Test hibernation by starting several applications, shut down to Hibernation mode, then restart the computer.**

   a. **Choose Start→All Programs→ Accessories→Calculator.**

   b. **Calculate 79 * 36.04, and leave Calculator open.**

   c. **Open Notepad and type** *Testing hibernation mode.* **Leave Notepad open.**

   d. **Open Disk Defragmenter, and click the C partition.**

   e. **Choose Action→Analyze.**

   f. In the Disk Defragmenter dialog box, **click Defragment.**

   g. While the Disk Defragmenter is running, **choose Start→Turn Off Computer.**

   h. **Place the mouse pointer over Stand By.**

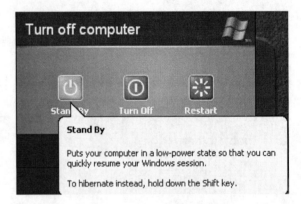

   i. **While pressing Shift, click Stand By.**

   j. **Restart the computer.**

   k. On the Welcome Screen, for your Admin## account, **type** *!Pass1234* **and click OK. Verify that Calculator, Notepad, and Disk Defragmenter are running.**

   l. **Close all applications and windows. You do not need to save any changes.**

Check Your Knowledge

1. Which devices in a laptop typically drain the most battery power?

   _____

   _____

2. How does power management help extend battery life?

   _____

   _____

   _____

   _____

   _____

3. What is the difference between hibernation and Stand By modes in Windows?

   _____

   _____

   _____

   _____

   _____

EXERCISE 12-3

Exchanging Portable Computer Drives

Setup:

To complete this activity, you will need a portable computer system that has a single drive bay with a floppy drive in it and a compatible CD/DVD drive.

 If the system you are using does not have drive bays for the floppy drive and CD or DVD drives, they are either in a docking solution or are attached using a cable. You will need to adapt this activity to match your system if this is the case.

Scenario:

Sally Mendez recently received a new portable computer. Her system has only one drive bay to use for the floppy drive and CD/DVD drive. The floppy drive is currently in the drive bay and she needs to use the CD/DVD drive. She is not sure how to remove the drive from her system.

 There is a simulated version of this activity available on the CD-ROM that shipped with this course. You can run this simulation on any Windows computer to review the activity after class, or as an alternative to performing the activity as a group in class. The activity simulation can be launched either directly from the CD-ROM by clicking the Interactives link and navigating to the appropriate one, or from the installed data file location by opening the C:\ 085820Data\Simulations\Lesson#\Activity# folder and double-clicking the executable (.exe) file.

What You Do	How You Do It
1. **Remove the floppy drive from the drive bay or cable connector.**	a. In the System Tray, **double-click the Safely Remove Hardware icon** to display a list of the devices that can be stopped.
	b. **Select the drive you want to remove.**
	c. **Click Stop** *drive description* (where *drive description* identifies the floppy drive you want to remove).
	d. In the Stop A Hardware Device information box, **click OK.**
	e. **Close the Safely Remove Hardware dialog box.**
	f. If the documentation specifies to, **shut down the system before continuing.**
	g. Referring to the documentation and any symbols on the system case, **locate the floppy drive and its release mechanism.**
	h. **Press the release mechanism for the floppy drive** to release it from the system.
	i. **Slide the floppy drive out of the drive bay or disconnect it from the cable.**
2. **Insert the CD/DVD drive in the bay or connect it to the cable.**	a. **Slide the CD/DVD drive into the drive bay or connect it to the cable.**
	b. If you had to shut down the system, **restart the system and log on.**
	c. **Verify that the Safely Remove Hardware icon appears in the System Tray.**
	d. **Access the CD/DVD drive** to verify that it was correctly installed.

Check Your Knowledge

1. Before removing any removable devices from a portable computer, what precautions must you take?

    _____

    _____

    _____

EXERCISE 12-4

Docking Portable Systems

Setup:

To complete this activity, you will need a portable computer and compatible port replicator or docking station.

Scenario:

Many members of the Marketing department have portable systems. They have all requested docking solutions for their systems so that they don't have to plug and unplug the external peripherals when they switch between working at desks in the office and working on the road or at home. The systems are from a variety of vendors. Some of the users have received port replicators and some have received docking stations. They need your assistance in connecting the external peripherals to the docking solutions and in how to insert and remove their portable systems from the docking solutions.

 There is a simulated version of this activity available on the CD-ROM that shipped with this course. You can run this simulation on any Windows computer to review the activity after class, or as an alternative to performing the activity as a group in class. The activity simulation can be launched either directly from the CD-ROM by clicking the Interactives link and navigating to the appropriate one, or from the installed data file location by opening the C:\085820Data\Simulations\Lesson#\Activity# folder and double-clicking the executable (.exe) file.

What You Do	How You Do It
1. Connect peripherals to the docking solution.	a. Connect the monitor to the monitor port on the docking solution.
	b. Connect the keyboard to the keyboard port on the docking solution.
	c. Connect the mouse to the mouse port on the docking solution.
	d. Connect the printer to the appropriate port for your printer on the docking solution.
	e. Connect the power source from the docking solution to the electrical outlet.

2. Verify that the portable system can use the peripherals while docked.

    a. **Insert the computer into the docking solution.**

    b. **Turn on the power.** This might be the power switch on the portable system or it might be a power switch on the docking solution.

    c. **Turn on the power to the monitor and to any other external peripherals that require powering on.**

    d. **Test that the external keyboard, mouse, monitor, and printer work properly.**

3. Verify that the portable system can use its integrated peripherals while undocked.

    a. **Turn off the power to all peripherals and to the portable system.**

    b. **Undock the system.**

    c. **Turn on the portable system and verify that the integrated keyboard, mouse, and monitor work correctly.**

Check Your Knowledge

1. What is the difference between connecting peripherals to a docking station versus directly to the laptop?

    _____

    _____

    _____

    _____

2. Is it necessary to power down the laptop before docking or undocking?

    _____

    _____

    _____

EXERCISE 12-5

Installing PC Cards

Setup:

To complete this activity, you will need a portable computer system with an empty PC Card slot and a compatible PC Card to insert.

Scenario:

Several users received new portable systems. These came with various expansion cards. You need to install the PC Cards so that the users can use them.

 There is a simulated version of this activity available on the CD-ROM that shipped with this course. You can run this simulation on any Windows computer to review the activity after class, or as an alternative to performing the activity as a group in class. The activity simulation can be launched either directly from the CD-ROM by clicking the Interactives link and navigating to the appropriate one, or from the installed data file location by opening the C:\085820Data\Simulations\Lesson#\Activity# folder and double-clicking the executable (.exe) file.

What You Do	How You Do It
1. Install the PC Card.	a. **Locate the PC Card slot on your portable system.**
	b. **Slide the PC Card into the slot until it is fully inserted.**
	c. If prompted, **install any required drivers for the PC Card.**

2. **Verify that the PC Card was recognized by the system.**

a. **Determine if an icon for the PC Card appeared in the System Tray.** Most cards will add an Unplug Or Eject Hardware icon.

b. **Open Device Manager.**

c. **Expand the appropriate device category and select the hardware you just installed.**

d. **Select the device and choose Action→ Properties.**

e. **Verify that Device Status indicates that This Device Is Working Properly.**

f. **Click OK.**

Check Your Knowledge

1. What precautions must you take when inserting PC cards into laptops?

_____

_____

_____

_____

_____

EXERCISE 12-6

Exchanging PC Cards

Setup:

To complete this activity, you will need a portable computer system with a PC Card slot that has a PC Card already installed and an additional, compatible PC Card to swap with the installed card.

Scenario:

Toby Macintosh has recently received a laptop system. The system has only one PC Card slot, but he has two compatible PC Cards. He would like your help in learning how to exchange the cards and to test them to verify that they work properly.

 There is a simulated version of this activity available on the CD-ROM that shipped with this course. You can run this simulation on any Windows computer to review the activity after class, or as an alternative to performing the activity as a group in class. The activity simulation can be launched either directly from the CD-ROM by clicking the Interactives link and navigating to the appropriate one, or from the installed data file location by opening the C:\ 085820Data\Simulations\Lesson#\Activity# folder and double-clicking the executable (.exe) file.

What You Do	How You Do It
1. **Remove the installed PC Card from the portable computer system.**	a. In the System Tray, **right-click the Safely Remove Hardware icon.**
	b. In the list of Hardware Devices, **select the device you want to remove and click Stop.**
	c. If the PC Card is a network card, **disconnect the network cable from the card.**
	d. **Push the PC Card slot release lever once** to pop it out.
	e. **Push the PC Card slot release lever again** to release the card from the slot.
	f. **Slide the card out of the slot.**

2. **Install the other PC Card in the portable computer system.**

   a. **Insert the other card in the PC Card slot.**

   b. If prompted, **install drivers for the other card.**

3. **Verify that the PC Card was recognized by the system.**

   a. **Determine if an icon for the PC Card appeared in the System Tray.** Most cards will add an Unplug Or Eject Hardware icon.

   b. **Open Device Manager.**

   c. **Expand the appropriate device category and select the hardware you just installed.**

   d. **Select the device and choose Action→ Properties.**

   e. **Verify that Device Status indicates that This Device Is Working Properly.**

   f. **Click OK.**

Check Your Knowledge

1. What is the proper procedure to remove a PC card from a laptop?

_____

_____

_____

EXERCISE 12-7

Installing a Mini-PCI Card

Setup:

To complete this activity, you will need a portable computer with a Mini-PCI bay and an extra Mini-PCI card.

Scenario:

You've been asked to add a new Mini-PCI card to a user's notebook computer. You know that this type of notebook has a dedicated Mini-PCI bay.

What You Do	How You Do It
1. Install the Mini-PCI card.	a. Shut down the system, close the cover, and unplug the power cord.
	b. If necessary, **remove the computer from the docking station or disconnect any peripheral devices.**
	c. Ground yourself and dissipate any static electricity you might be carrying.
	d. Turn over the laptop and follow the manufacturer's instructions to locate the Mini-PCI bay cover.
	e. Remove the screw that secures the Mini-PCI bay cover.
	f. Remove the Mini-PCI bay cover.
	g. Secure the card inside the bay using the supplied screws or clamps.
	h. Replace the cover on the bay and fasten it with the screw.

2. **Verify that the card is installed properly.**

   a. **Plug in the computer or replace it in the docking station.**

   b. **Turn on the power.**

   c. **Verify that the new Mini-PCI card has been recognized.** If necessary, **install any updated drivers.**

Check Your Knowledge

1. What is the difference between installing a Mini-PCI card and a PC card in a laptop?

2. What procedures must you follow when installing a Mini-PCI card in a laptop?

EXERCISE 12-8

Adding Memory to Portable Computing Devices

Setup:

To complete this activity, you need a portable computing device with an empty memory slot and a compatible memory chip.

Scenario:

You have just received the memory modules that were ordered for several portable computing devices. You need to deploy them to the devices for users.

 There is a simulated version of this activity available on the CD-ROM that shipped with this course. You can run this simulation on any Windows computer to review the activity after class, or as an alternative to performing the activity as a group in class. The activity simulation can be launched either directly from the CD-ROM by clicking the Interactives link and navigating to the appropriate one, or from the installed data file location by opening the C:\ 085820Data\Simulations\Lesson#\Activity# folder and double-clicking the executable (.exe) file.

What You Do	How You Do It
1. **Install memory in a portable computer.**	a. **Shut down and unplug the portable computer.**

 This may not always be a required step. Some portable devices do not require you to shut the system down before inserting memory. Check the manufacturer's instructions before you start to determine how to proceed.

    b. **Locate and remove the memory cover on the case.**

    c. **Verify that the memory module you are about to install matches the specifications for the memory slot.**

    d. Following the directions in the documentation, **install the memory module.**

    e. **Replace and secure the cover to the memory.**

    f. **Restart the computer.**

    g. **Verify that the additional memory was recognized.**

2. **Install a memory module in an MP3 player, a PDA, or a digital camera.**

    a. **Turn off the device.**

    b. **Locate the expansion slot for the memory card.**

    c. If necessary, **remove the existing memory card.**

    d. **Verify that the memory card matches the specifications for adding memory to the device.**

    e. **Insert the memory card into the slot.**

    f. **Turn on the device.**

    g. **Verify that the memory was recognized.**

Check Your Knowledge

1. Is laptop memory the same as desktop computer memory?

_____

_____

_____

2. How can you expand a PDA or digital device's memory?

_____

_____

_____

_____

EXERCISE 12-9

Connecting Infrared Devices

Setup:

You can complete this activity only if you have an infrared device and computer with an infrared port or to which you can add an infrared port.

Scenario:

The head of the Marketing department uses wireless devices in order to keep her desk clear from cables. She has a wireless mouse, keyboard, PDA, and printer. She has asked you to set up her equipment.

 There is a simulated version of this activity available on the CD-ROM that shipped with this course. You can run this simulation on any Windows computer to review the activity after class, or as an alternative to performing the activity as a group in class. The activity simulation can be launched either directly from the CD-ROM by clicking the Interactives link and navigating to the appropriate one, or from the installed data file location by opening the C:\085820Data\Simulations\Lesson#\Activity# folder and double-clicking the executable (.exe) file.

What You Do	How You Do It
1. Position each device and the computer so that you can make the connection between the wireless device and the computer.	a. Power on the computer and the device.
	b. Position the devices so there is a direct line of sight between the two infrared ports.

2. Configure the device as appropriate to the system.

    a. If you are connecting an infrared device to a serial or USB port, **open Control Panel, and then click Add Hardware.**

    b. **Click Next.**

    c. **Click Add A New Hardware Device, and then click Next.**

    d. **Select Install The Hardware That I Manually Select From A List, and then click Next.**

    e. **Select Infrared Devices, and then click Next.**

    f. If you have a driver for the device, **click Have Disk, and then click Next.**

    If you don't have a driver for the device, **select the manufacturer and device that match your device, and then click Next.**

    g. **Click Next.**

    h. **Select the port your infrared device is attached to, and then click Next.**

3. Transfer data between the devices.

    a. **Position the devices with a direct line of sight between the infrared port on the computer and the wireless device.**

    b. Following the directions in the device documentation, **transfer data between the devices.**

Check Your Knowledge

1. What are some of the limitations of infrared connectivity?

_____

_____

_____

_____

_____

2. How can you adjust infrared settings and configure connectivity options?

_____

_____

EXERCISE 12-10

Connecting Bluetooth Devices

Setup:

You can complete this activity only if you have a Bluetooth device and a computer that is Bluetooth-enabled or to which you can add a Bluetooth port.

Scenario:

A user has asked you to configure his new Bluetooth PDA to communicate with his computer.

 There is a simulated version of this activity available on the CD-ROM that shipped with this course. You can run this simulation on any Windows computer to review the activity after class, or as an alternative to performing the activity as a group in class. The activity simulation can be launched either directly from the CD-ROM by clicking the Interactives link and navigating to the appropriate one, or from the installed data file location by opening the C:\ 085820Data\Simulations\Lesson#\Activity# folder and double-clicking the executable (.exe) file.

What You Do	How You Do It
1. On the Bluetooth device, **enable Bluetooth connectivity.**	a. If necessary, **turn on Bluetooth.**
	b. If necessary, **configure a device name and enable the device to be discoverable.**
	c. **Add your computer to the list of trusted devices on the Bluetooth device.**
2. If necessary, **install a Bluetooth adapter in your computer.**	a. If you are using a Bluetooth USB adapter, **plug the adapter into an open USB port.**
	b. **Verify that Windows XP successfully installs the adapter's drivers.**
	c. If necessary, **use Device Manager to install the manufacturer's drivers for the Bluetooth adapter.**

3. **Configure the Bluetooth settings on the computer.**

a. In Control Panel, **click the Printers And Other Hardware link.**

b. **Click Bluetooth Devices.**

c. **Click the Options tab.**

d. **Check the Turn Discovery On check box and then click Apply.**

e. **Click Add.** On the Welcome page, **check the My Device Is Set Up And Ready To Be Found check box, and then click Next.**

f. In the list of discovered Bluetooth devices, **select the device you want to add and click Next.**

g. **Verify that Choose A Passkey For Me is selected and then click Next.**

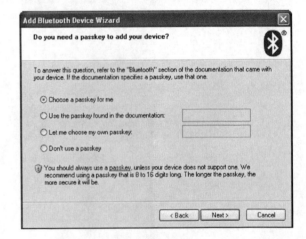

h. On the Bluetooth device, **enter the passkey.**

i. On the computer, when prompted enter the passkey.

 Your steps will vary depending on the Bluetooth device.

		j.	On the computer, to complete the Bluetooth setup, **click Finish.**
4.	If necessary, **install any Bluetooth device-specific software on your computer.**	a.	**Insert the installation CD.**
		b.	**Follow the prompts in the installation wizard.**
5.	**Verify that both the computer and the Bluetooth device can see each other.**	a.	On the computer, **verify that you see the Bluetooth device listed in the Bluetooth Devices dialog box.**

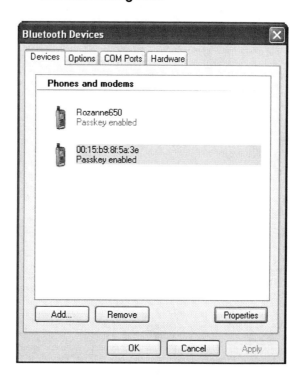

	b.	On the Bluetooth device, **verify that you can see the computer listed.**

Check Your Knowledge

1. What must you do before attempting to establish communication between a portable device and a desktop computer using Bluetooth wireless connectivity?

_____

_____

_____

2. Which Bluetooth setting allows your device to be detected by other Bluetooth-enabled devices?

    _____

3. How can you better secure your Bluetooth connection to prevent unauthorized access to your device?

    _____

    _____

EXERCISE 12-11

Discussing Laptop and Portable Computing Device Troubleshooting

Scenario:

In this activity, you will discuss troubleshooting issues for laptops and portable computing devices.

---

1. **Which mobile component has specific maintenance techniques that are not normally used for desktop computers?**

   a) Keyboards and pointing devices

   b) LCD screens

   c) Cooling systems

   d) Batteries

---

2. **Identify which components are typically soldered to the system board and cannot be replaced without replacing the entire system board.**

   a) Fan

   b) Processor

   c) USB port

   d) PCMCIA bay

   e) AC adapter connection

---

3. **Identify which components are typically connected to the system board and can be replaced independently of the system board.**

   a) Hard disk

   b) Infrared port

   c) External monitor port

   d) Fan

   e) Keyboard

---

4. **A user complains her mobile device is hot to the touch. What action would you take to investigate this issue?**

   a) Clean the ventilation duct with compressed air.

   b) Replace the battery.

   c) Adjust the screen brightness.

   d) Make sure the machine gets proper air circulation.

---

5. **A PDA user is complaining that the touch screen of her device is not responding to the stylus correctly. When she places the stylus on the screen, the cursor is placed nearly an inch to the left. How would you resolve this issue?**

    a) Try another stylus

    b) Calibrate the touch screen in the device's operating system.

    c) Replace the protective film on the screen.

    d) Restart the device.

6. **What other types of problems have you experienced with laptops and portable computing devices? How did you solve the problems?**

Check Your Knowledge

1. When troubleshooting laptop components, which components typically cannot be replaced without replacing the system board?

2. Which laptop components can be typically replaced because they are independent of the system board?

3. How would you troubleshoot a PDA touch screen that is not responding to user input?

LAB 12-1

Supporting Portable Computing Devices

Activity Time: 30 minutes

Scenario:

 You can find a suggested solution for this activity in the Solutions\Supporting Portable Computing Devices.txt file in the data file location.

---

1.   **Set up the notebook computer.**

---

2.   **Set up the docking solution connecting all of the desktop components the user will use through it while the notebook is docked.**

---

3.   **Set up the PDA.**

---

4.   **Install the PDA software on the computer.**

---

5.   **Connect the digital camera to the notebook or insert the flash media in the PDA.**

---

6.   **Connect the MP3 player to the computer.**

13 | Supporting Printers and Scanners

Activities included in this chapter:

- Exercise 13-1 Discussing Printer and Scanner Technologies
- Exercise 13-2 Identifying Printer and Scanner Components
- Exercise 13-3 Discussing Printer and Scanner Processes
- Exercise 13-4 Installing a Local Printer
- Exercise 13-5 Verifying the Printer Installation
- Exercise 13-6 Troubleshooting Printing Problems
- Exercise 13-7 Performing Printer Maintenance
- Lab 13-1 Troubleshooting Printer Problems

EXERCISE 13-1

Discussing Printer and Scanner Technologies

Scenario:

In this activity, you will discuss major printer and scanner technology categories.

1. **What type of scanner is this?**

 a) Flatbed scanner

 b) Handheld scanner

 c) Sheetfed scanner

 d) Three-dimensional scanner

2. **Which functions are typically provided by a multi-function device?**

 a) Scanning

 b) Printing

 c) Faxing

 d) Audio playback

 e) Copying

3. **Match the printer type with its description**

___	Laser printer	a. Uses heat to create images.
___	Inkjet printer	b. Melts a waxy stick and forces the liquid into a printhead and onto paper
___	Thermal printer	c. Forms images by direct contact between a printer component and the paper
___	Solid ink printer	d. Creates high-quality images using toner and an intense beam of light.
___	Impact printer	e. Forms images by spraying liquid from a cartridge through a nozzle.

4. **Match the thermal printer type with its description.**

___	Dye sublimation printer	a. Uses heated pins to form images on coated paper.
___	Thermal wax transfer printer	b. A sophisticated color that produces photo-quality continuous-tone images.
___	Direct thermal printer	c. A printer that melts ink from a transfer ribbon onto paper to produce acceptable-quality color output in standard office environments.

5. **What are the two main types of impact printers?**

Check Your Knowledge

1. What are the different types of scanners you may encounter in the field?

    _____

    _____

    _____

    _____

2. What are the typical functions you will find in most office multi-function devices (MFD)?

    _____

    _____

3. Which type of printer can be used to print multi-part forms with several carbon copies?

    _____

    _____

    _____

4. List the most common printer technologies you will encounter in the field.

EXERCISE 13-2

Identifying Printer and Scanner Components

Scenario:

In this activity, you will identify hardware and software components that are used in many printers and scanners.

---

1. **Which are functions of printer memory?**

   a) To store information about current device settings.

   b) To store scanned images.

   c) To store service manuals.

   d) To store print jobs in a queue.

---

2. **What is the function of printer or scanner firmware?**

   a) To communicate with the computer system.

   b) To communicate with the network.

   c) To provide the on-board management interface for the device.

   d) To store information about the current print job or scanned image.

---

3. **Which of the following are consumable components for printers or scanners?**

   a) Paper or transparency stock

   b) Centronics connectors

   c) Memory

   d) Toner

   e) Ink cartridges or sticks

---

4. **What is the function of the printer or scanner driver?**

   a) To provide the on-board device management interface.

   b) To control device-specific functions.

   c) To provide sophisticated control funcitons.

   d) To provide network access to the device.

Check Your Knowledge

1. When sending a print job to a printer, where is the job stored prior to the actual printing?

   _____

   _____

   _____

   _____

2. What are consumable components? What are examples of consumable components for printers?

   _____

   _____

   _____

3. What function does a printer's firmware serve?

   _____

   _____

EXERCISE 13-3

Discussing Printer and Scanner Processes

Scenario:
In this activity, you will discuss printer and scanner processes.

---

1. **In which process is the EP drum given a strong negative charge?**

   a) The laser print process.

   b) The inkjet print process.

   c) The solid ink print process.

   d) The impact print process.

   e) The scanning process.

---

2. **In which process does the stabilizer bar move from one end of the source to the other?**

   a) The laser print process.

   b) The inkjet print process.

   c) The solid ink print process.

   d) The impact print process.

   e) The scanning process.

---

3. **In which process is ink forced out of nozzles onto the paper?**

   a) The laser print process.

   b) The inkjet print process.

   c) The solid ink print process.

   d) The impact print process.

   e) The scanner process.

---

4. **In which process are pins controlled by an electromagnet?**

   a) The laser print process.

   b) The inkjet print process.

   c) The solid ink print process.

   d) The impact print process.

   e) The scanner process.

Check Your Knowledge

1. What are the steps in the laser printing process?

   _____

   _____

2. What is the purpose of the fusing step in the laser printing process?

   _____

   _____

3. What are the two types of inkjet printings you will encounter in the field?

   _____

   _____

4. What are the steps in the inkjet printing process?

   _____

EXERCISE 13-4

Installing a Local Printer

Setup:

Simple File Sharing has been disabled. If Simple File Sharing is enabled on your system, disable it before starting the activity; in the Printers And Faxes window, choose Tools→Folder Options, click View, and uncheck Use Simple File Sharing.

Scenario:

One of your clients has just asked you to install a refurbished Hewlett-Packard Color Laserjet 5 that he purchased online. He would like to use this printer on his Windows XP computer as his default printer. Your client's computer has a single parallel port. He has also asked that you make the printer available to other users in the company. Even though your client hasn't yet received the printer, he would like you to configure his computer so that all he will need to do is plug in the printer when it arrives.

There is a simulated version of this activity available on the CD-ROM that shipped with this course. You can run this simulation on any Windows computer to review the activity after class, or as an alternative to performing the activity as a group in class. The activity simulation can be launched either directly from the CD-ROM by clicking the Interactives link and navigating to the appropriate one, or from the installed data file location by opening the C:\ 085820Data\Simulations\Lesson#\Activity# folder and double-clicking the executable (.exe) file.

What You Do	How You Do It
1. Install the printer.	a. **Choose Start→Printers And Faxes.**
	b. Under Printer Tasks, **click Add A Printer.**
	c. In the Add Printer Wizard, **click Next.**
	d. **Verify that Local Printer Attached To This Computer is selected. Uncheck Automatically Detect And Install My Plug And Play Printer and click Next.**

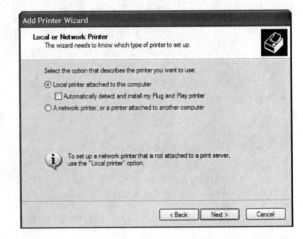

	e. Next to Use The Following Port, **verify that LPT1 is selected and click Next.**
	f. Below Manufacturer, **scroll down and select HP.**
	g. Below Printers, **scroll down and select HP Color LaserJet 5.**
	h. **Click Next.**
	i. For the Printer Name, **type Color##,** where ## is your student number.
	j. If necessary, under Do You Want To Use This Printer As The Default Printer, **verify that Yes is selected and click Next.**
2. Share the printer and complete the installation.	a. **Select Share Name.**

   b. **Verify that the Share Name is *Color##*, and click Next.**

   c. On the Location And Comment page, **click Next.**

   d. Below Do You Want To Print A Test Page, **select No and click Next.**

   e. **Click Finish.**

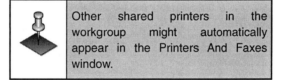

> Other shared printers in the workgroup might automatically appear in the Printers And Faxes window.

   f. **Verify that the shared printer appears in the Printers And Faxes window.**

Color04
0
Ready

Check Your Knowledge

1. How can you share your printer with other users on the network?

_____

_____

_____

EXERCISE 13-5

Verifying the Printer Installation

Scenario:
You've just set up some shared printers on a Windows XP Professional computer so that you can use it as a print server for your workgroup. You want to do a test run on the new print server and make sure that all the print process components on the system are present and functioning correctly.

 There is a simulated version of this activity available on the CD-ROM that shipped with this course. You can run this simulation on any Windows computer to review the activity after class, or as an alternative to performing the activity as a group in class. The activity simulation can be launched either directly from the CD-ROM by clicking the Interactives link and navigating to the appropriate one, or from the installed data file location by opening the C:\085820Data\Simulations\Lesson#\Activity# folder and double-clicking the executable (.exe) file.

What You Do	How You Do It
1. **Create a print job on your local printer.**	a. In the Printers And Faxes window, **select the printer object and choose File→ Pause Printing.**
	b. **Choose File→Properties.**
	c. **Click Print Test Page.**
	d. **Click OK twice.**
	e. **Double-click the printer object to open the print queue window.**
	f. At least one print job should appear in the queue. **Close the print queue window.**

2. Identify the print driver files for your printer.

a. In the Printers And Faxes window, **choose File→Server Properties.**

b. **Click the Drivers tab.**

c. In the Installed Printer Drivers list, **verify that the the HP Color LaserJet 5 driver is selected and click Properties.**

d. There are several separate files that make up the complete driver. Although not visible on screen, the full driver path is C:\Windows\System32\Spool\Drivers\ W32X86\3. The "3" indicates drivers for the Windows XP Professional platform; drivers for earlier versions of Windows would be stored in differently numbered subdirectories. **Click Close.**

e. **Click OK.**

3. Identify the spooler service.

a. In the Printers And Faxes window, in the task pane, under Other Places, **right-click My Computer and choose Manage.**

b. **Expand Services And Applications.**

c. **Select Services.**

d. **Scroll to view the Print Spooler Service.**

e. **Verify that the service Startup Type is Automatic and close Computer Management.**

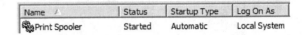

Name	Status	Startup Type	Log On As
Print Spooler	Started	Automatic	Local System

4. **Identify the spool file directory.**

a. In the Printers And Faxes window, **choose File→Server Properties.**

b. **Click the Advanced tab.**

c. The spool folder location appears in the Spool Folder text box. The files containing spooled print jobs are stored in this folder. You can type a new spool folder location if you wish. **Click Cancel.**

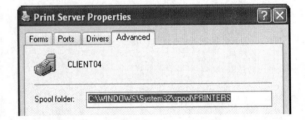

5. **Verify the default printer permissions.**

    a. With the printer object selected, **choose File→Properties.**

    b. **Click the Security tab.**

    c. In the Group Or User Names list, **select the Everyone group.**

    d. **Verify that Everyone is allowed the Print permission and click OK.**

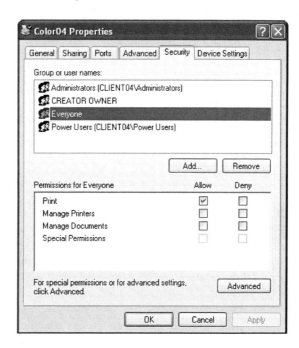

    e. **Close the Printers And Faxes window.**

Check Your Knowledge

1. What function does the Print Spooler service serve?

2. What are the components of the Printing Spooler?

3. Where is the Printing Spooler folder usually located?

EXERCISE 13-6

Troubleshooting Printing Problems

Scenario:

You're contracted as an A+ technician to work on-site at one of your client's locations. The client has asked you to manage all of the printers on the network. You're responsible for responding to any problems that arise with printing. While you were out at lunch, you received some trouble tickets relating to printing problems.

---

1. Mary reports that she's unable to print from Microsoft Excel. After talking with her on the phone, you've determined that everything is fine with the printer hardware. When you get to her desk, what step should you take next to troubleshoot the problem?

---

2. Julie calls you on the phone and proceeds to explain that she just received her new scanner in the mail. She connected the power cord to the outlet and installed the device software on the computer. When she starts up the scanner, nothing happens. What is the first thing you should check once you get to Julie's desk?

---

3. Andy reports that he's attempting to print to his local printer, but none of the print jobs are printing. When you arrive at his desk, you check out the printer hardware and everything seems to be fine. When you double-click the printer in the Printers folder, you see Andy's jobs listed in the queue. What should you try next?

---

4. Eduardo says all of his printouts look garbled. You check the properties of the print object in the Printers and Faxes window and find that the printer model listed in the Properties dialog box is not the same as the printer model on the printer itself. What should you do?

---

5. **Sheila Wright says the dot matrix printer she uses for printing multi-part forms was printing poorly. What is the most likely solution to this problem?**

    a) Replace the toner cartridge.

    b) Clean the print head.

    c) Replace the ink cartridge.

    d) Replace the ribbon.

6. **Toni Mancuso reports that inkjet printers in the corporate training area have various problems, including no output, fuzzy output, and generally poor print quality. List some of the steps you should take when resolving these problems.**

7. **Suzanne's computer is configured to print to both a local and a network printer. She just installed a old non-Windows application and executed the command net use lpt1 \\printserv\netprint so that she can print from the non-Windows application. Suzanne reports that all her print jobs now print to the network printer. What might be the problem and how can you fix it?**

Check Your Knowledge

1. What diagnostic tool can you use to test printer functionality, even when the printer is not connected to any computer?

2. A user's print jobs are sitting in the print queue and not being printed. What would you try next?

_____

_____

_____

3. A dot matrix printer is not printing the top form clearly; however, the duplicates are clear. How would you resolve this issue?

_____

_____

4. How would you address a problem in which and inkjet printer is printing poorly, including smearing ink and fuzzy characters and images?

_____

_____

_____

_____

_____

_____

_____

EXERCISE 13-7

Performing Printer Maintenance

Scenario:

In this activity, you will examine the hardware for your classroom printer or printers and perform printer maintenance using maintenance supplies your instructor will provide. Your instructor may choose to introduce various printer problems for you to resolve.

1. Follow your instructor's directions to examine the internal components of your classroom printer or printers.

2. Resolve any problems that exist with the printers.

3. Perform any appropriate maintenance tasks for your printer.

4. Which device requires that you use a soft cloth and cleaner to clean its glass bed of any smudges or marks?

   a) Scanner

   b) Laser printer

   c) Inkjet printer

   d) Thermal printer

5. What are the general steps taken to maintain a printer or scanner?

   Clean and organize the area around the device to make sure it is free from clutter. Make sure there isn't anything on top of the device.

   Using the vendor-recommended cleaner, dust around the area of the device.

   Check the device's plugs and cords to make sure they are secured to the power source and to the device.

   Perform the regular maintenance tasks that are recommended by the specific vendor of the device.

6. True or False? While cleaning an impact printer, you should use a vacuum to clean out the paper shaft.

   ___ True

   ___ False

LAB 13-1

Troubleshooting Printer Problems

Activity Time: 20 minutes

Scenario:

 You can find suggested solutions for this activity in the \Solutions\Troubleshooting Printer Problems.txt file in the data file location.

1. After each problem situation has been set up in the printing environment, **use Notepad to print a document to the default printer.**

2. After determining the current problem situation, **diagnose the print problem by determining the nature, extent, and cause of the problem.**

3. **Correct each print problem, reprint the document, and verify that it appears in the print queue or that the physical output appears at the print device.**

4. **Repeat these steps as needed to resolve other problem situations.**

14 Personal Computer Security Concepts

Activities included in this chapter:

- Exercise 14-1 Discussing Security Fundamentals
- Exercise 14-2 Discussing Security Protection Measures
- Exercise 14-3 Discussing Data and Physical Security
- Exercise 14-4 Discussing Wireless Security
- Exercise 14-5 Identifying Social Engineering Attacks
- Exercise 14-6 Responding to Social Engineering Attacks
- Lab 14-1 Discussing Security Fundamentals

EXERCISE 14-1

Discussing Security Fundamentals

Scenario:
In this activity, you will discuss the fundamentals of computer security.

1. A formalized statement that defines how security will be implemented in a particular organization is called:

   a) An incident report.

   b) A security policy.

   c) An authentication method.

   d) A token.

2. Katie works in a high-security government facility. When she comes to work in the morning, she places her hand on a scanning device in her building's lobby, which reads her handprint and compares it to a master record of her handprint in a database to verify her identity. This is an example of:

   a) Biometric authentication.

   b) Multi-factor authentication.

   c) Data encryption.

   d) Tokens.

3. Which are characteristics of biometric authentication?

   a) It can be more expensive than other authentication schemes.

   b) It involves the use of a token.

   c) In theory, it is highly secure.

   d) It is based on physical characteristics.

   e) It eliminates the need for passwords.

4. Match the access control method on the left to the correct description on the right.

   ____ Mandatory Access Control (MAC)

   a. The access to each object is controlled on a customized basis based on a user's identity.

   ____ Discretionary Access Control (DAC)

   b. The access is controlled by comparing an object's security designation and a user's security clearance.

   ____ Role-based Access Control (RBAC)

   c. Users are assigned to pre-defined roles, and network objects are configuredto allow access only to specific roles.

5. **Which are the most powerful user accounts for Windows XP?**

   a) Administrator

   b) An account created during installation

   c) Guest

   d) Support

6. **A disgruntled employee wants to delete some key company data from his computer system. Before doing so, he tries to change the computer system time to make it look as if the damage occurred at a time when he was not present. He receives a message "You are not authorized to change the system time. Please contact your administrator." This is an example of what security mechanism?**

   a) Permissions

   b) Encryption

   c) A firewall

   d) Rights

7. **The function that tracks user and operating system activities by recording selected types of events in the security log of a computer is called:**

   a) Authentication

   b) Access control

   c) Auditing

   d) Password management

Check Your Knowledge

1. What are the three access control methods you need to be aware of when discussing access control implementation?

   _____

   _____

2. What is biometric authentication?

   _____

   _____

   _____

3. What are some of the limitations of biometric authentication?

   _____

   _____

4. What is a security policy?

_____

_____

5. How can auditing help maintain security?

_____

_____

_____

EXERCISE 14-2

Discussing Security Protection Measures

Scenario:
In this activity, you will discuss general security protection measures you can take to safeguard your network.

---

1. Alice sends a message to Bob. Inside the message is a small, coded piece of information that proves that Alice was the message sender. This is an example of:

    a) Hashing.

    b) Symmetric encryption.

    c) Asymmetric encryption.

    d) Block cipher.

---

2. Alice sends a coded message to Bob. Before she does, she sends Bob a copy of the mathematical formula she used to encrypt the message so that he can decrypt it when he receives it. This is an example of:

    a) Hashing.

    b) Symmetric encryption.

    c) Asymmetric encryption.

    d) Block cipher.

---

3. Alice uses a piece of information that she obtains from a database to send a coded message to Bob. Bob uses a piece of information that only he knows to decode the message. This is an example of:

    a) Hashing.

    b) Symmetric encryption.

    c) Asymmetric encryption.

    d) Block cipher.

---

4. What security mechanism would you apply if you wanted to protect the contents of network data packets while they are in transit?

    a) Authentication

    b) File system permissions

    c) Encryption

    d) A firewall

---

5. **Match the type of malicious software with its description.**

___ Virus

___ Logic bomb

___ Spam

___ Spyware

___ Trojan

___ Grayware

a. Any unwanted software that produces harmful or annoying effects.

b. Monitors system activities and sends private data to a third party.

c. Propagates by attaching itself to other files.

d. Sits dormant until triggered by a specific event.

e. Floods mail boxes and mail servers with unsolicited or distasteful messages.

f. Masquerades as a legitimate program while performing unauthorized operations.

6. **True or False? The only negative effect of a virus hoax is increased network traffic.**

___ True

___ False

7. **True or False? The safest way to deal with unsolicited email is to delete it without opening it.**

___ True

___ False

8. **Shortly after signing up for online banking at your financial institution, you receive an email requesting that you reconfirm your name, address, taxpayer identification information, and account number. What should you do?**

   a) Assume that your information was lost, and resubmit it by replying to the email.

   b) Assume that your information was lost, and resubmit it by clicking a link in the email.

   c) Report the incident to the company. Also, check the financial institution's website for security alerts regarding fraudulent emails.

   d) Cancel the online account, and reapply using a different email address.

Check Your Knowledge

1. List some of the more common malicious software.

_____

_____

2. What is data encryption?

_____

_____

3. How can you protect a network from attacks originating somewhere on the Internet?

_____

4. What is one of the most important things that can be done to protect a system against malicious software?

_____

_____

_____

5. Identify the three main techniques for encrypting data.

_____

_____

EXERCISE 14-3

Discussing Data and Physical Security

Scenario:

In this activity, you will identify security measures you can take to protect computer data and physical computer systems.

---

1. **Match the backup security measure with a security threat it can protect against.**

    ___ A vandal destroying the backup tapes.

    ___ Backup tapes destroyed by a warehouse fire.

    ___ A hacker overwriting current user data with old data.

    ___ A malicious employing making unauthorized backup copies and selling the tapes to a competitor.

    a. Employ strict policies to control who can perform backup operations.

    b. Restrict physical access to the backup storage location.

    c. Employ strict policies to control who can perform restore operations.

    d. Keep at least two copies of backup tapes.

---

2. **You need to send a sensitive data document to a colleague who works for a partner company. What methods would help ensure that you transfer this information securely?**

    a) Copy the data from the document into the email and send it in plain text.

    b) Use a compression program on the document, assign a password to the compressed file, and send the email with the compressed file as an attachment.

    c) Attach the document and use an email encryption protocol to send the message.

    d) Read the document to your colleague over the phone.

---

3. **A user is upgrading the hard disk in her desktop computer. The old hard disk does not meet your current hardware standards so you will not reuse it. What steps are appropriate to transfer the data and dispose of the old disk?**

    a) Transfer the data from the old hard disk to the new with a direct connection.

    b) Reformat the old hard disk one time.

    c) Bulk erase the old hard disk.

    d) Dispose of the old hard disk with a computer hardware recycling contractor.

    e) Throw the old hard disk in the trash.

---

4. **As part of a new job position, you are required to travel to the home office for training, but you also need to keep current with email and other project communications. What can you do to secure your laptop when you are traveling?**

   a) Leave the laptop at home.

   b) Use a locking cable to secure the laptop to hotel furniture.

   c) Encrypt sensitive data on the system.

   d) Delete all sensitive information from the laptop before you leave.

Check Your Knowledge

1. What is backup security and how is it important to the safety of a company's data?

2. What are some things that you can do to ensure that old storage media is safely disposed of?

3. How can you protect portable devices to prevent unauthorized access?

4. What preventive measures can you take before transporting sensitive data from one location to another, whether physically transporting the data or sending it electronically?

EXERCISE 14-4

Discussing Wireless Security

Scenario:
In this activity, you will discuss wireless security concepts.

1. **Match each wireless security protocol with the description.**

   ___ WEP

   ___ WTLS

   ___ 802.1x

   ___ WPA
   ___ 802.11i

   a. A security protocol using stream cipher data encryption that provides dynamic reassignment of keys.

   b. A data-encryption method with a flawed key-generation algorithm.

   c. A wireless standard using AES data encryption.

   d. The security layer of WAP.

   e. A wireless authentication mechanism using EAP.

2. **Select the appropriate measures to take to secure wireless traffic.**

   a) Implement a security protocol for data encryption.

   b) Implement strong access control and authentication.

   c) Use only WEP-compatible devices.

   d) Keep current with software patches and firmware updates.

   e) Use only WAP-compatible devices.

Check Your Knowledge

1. How can you secure communication on your wireless network?

   _____

2. What measures can you take to prevent unauthorized access to a wireless network?

   _____

   _____

   _____

EXERCISE 14-5

Identifying Social Engineering Attacks

Scenario:
In this activity, you will identify social engineering attacks.

---

1. **Social engineering attempt or false alarm?** A supposed customer calls the help desk stating that she cannot connect to the e-commerce website to check order status. She would also like a user name and password. The user gives a valid customer company name, but is not listed as a contact in the customer database. The user doesn't know the correct company code or customer ID.

   __ Social engineering attempt

   __ False alarm

---

2. **Social engineering attempt or false alarm?** The VP of Sales is in the middle of a presentation to a group of key customers and accidentally logs off. She urgently needs to continue with the presentation, but forgot her password. You recognize her voice on the line, but she is supposed to have her boss make the request according to the company password security policy.

   __ Social engineering attempt

   __ False alarm

---

3. **Social engineering attempt or false alarm?** A new accountant was hired and would like to know if he can have the installation CD-ROM for the accounting software package, so that he can install it on his computer himself and start work immediately. Last year, someone internal compromised company accounting records, so distribution of the accounting application is tightly controlled. You have received all the proper documentation for the request from his supervisor and there is an available license for the software. However, general IT policies state that the IT department must perform all software installations and upgrades.

   __ Social engineering attempt

   __ False alarm

---

4. **Social engineering attempt or false alarm?** Christine receives a message in her instant messaging software asking for her account and password. The person sending the message states that the request comes from the IT department, because they need to do a backup of Christine's local hard drive.

   __ Social engineering attempt

   __ False alarm

---

5. **Social engineering attempt or false alarm? Rachel gets an email with an attachment that is named NewVirusDefinitions.vbs. The name in the email is the same as the IT software manager, but the email address is from an account outside the company.**

    ___ Social engineering attempt

    ___ False alarm

6. **Social engineering attempt or false alarm? A user calls the help desk stating that he is a phone technician needing the password to configure the phone and voice mail system.**

    ___ Social engineering attempt

    ___ False alarm

7. **Social engineering attempt or false alarm? A vendor team requests access to the building to fix an urgent problem with a piece of equipment. Although the team has no work order and the guard was not notified of the visit, the team is wearing shirts and hats from the preferred vendor. The guard lets the vendor team through without a required escort.**

    ___ Social engineering attempt

    ___ False alarm

8. **Social engineering attempt or false alarm? The CEO of the organization needs to get access to market research data immediately. You definitely recognize her voice, but a proper request form hasn't been filled out to modify the permissions. She states that normally she would fill out the form and should not be an exception, but she urgently needs the data.**

    ___ Social engineering attempt

    ___ False alarm

9. **In the midst of editing a document, an unfamiliar message appears on your screen. It says that your network connection has been dropped and that you need to log on again. Could this be a possible exploit attempt?**

    a) Yes

    b) No

    c) Only on a coporate network

    d) Only on a dial-up connection

10. **Your team has a deadline and is again working late into the evening. You return from a short dinner break to find someone wearing a janitor's uniform in your work area. You've never seen this person before, but she has an ID tag clipped to her pocket. What would make you think this is a possible exploit attempt?**

    a) She has a uniform and an ID tag.

    b) She is a stranger in your work area.

    c) She is there late in the evening.

11. **Returning from lunch with a coworker, you use your swipe card to unlock the employee entrance. Your coworker mentions that it's a good thing she had lunch with you because she left her swipe card in her other jacket. Is this a possible exploit?**

___ Yes

___ No

12. **A support technician for your Internet Service Provider calls you at home with a limited offer. If you provide your user name and password, you'll get a free account upgrade. What would make you think this is a possible exploit attempt?**

a) Asking for your name and password.

b) The special offer from the ISP.

c) Being called at home.

Check Your Knowledge

1. What is a social engineering attack and how does it affect the security and privacy of information?

_____

_____

_____

_____

2. What is phishing and how is it relevant to data security?

_____

_____

3. How can social engineering attacks be mitigated or prevented?

_____

_____

EXERCISE 14-6

Responding to Social Engineering Attacks

Scenario:

In this activity, you will discuss ways to respond to social engineering attacks. Remember, all responses should also conform to the organizational security policies.

1. **You get a call from someone identifying himself as a new support technician for your organization. He tells you that if you provide your user name and password, he will update your account so that you can take advantage of additional network resources. What should you do?**

   a) Take down his name and number, and tell him you'll call back. Then, report the incident.

   b) Provide the requested information.

   c) Take down his name and number, and tell him you'll call him back. Then, call back and provide the requested information.

2. **In the midst of composing an email, an unfamiliar pop-up appears on your screen, indicating that your email connection has been dropped and you need to log on again by using the pop-up screen. What should you do?**

   a) Complete the screen and submit the information.

   b) Report the incident without submitting the information.

   c) Ignore and close the pop-up without notifying anyone.

   d) Report the incident after submitting the information.

   e) Restart your email client.

3. **A phone technician calls explaining that he is working on the system, but needs an outside line to call home because he got an urgent page from his daughter. What should you do?**

   a) Refuse the request and report the incident.

   b) Transfer the call as requested.

   c) Transfer the call to the switchboard.

4. **Your team has a deadline and is working late into the evening. You return from a short dinner break to find someone wearing a janitor's uniform in your work area. Although you work late quite often, you've never seen this person before. What should you do?**

   a) Ignore her and get back to work.

   b) Ask to see her identification.

   c) Demand that she leave the area.

Check Your Knowledge

1. When faced with a possible social engineering attack, what can you do to minimize its impact?

   _____

   _____

   _____

2. What is an appropriate initial response to an unfamiliar request for access, passwords, or privileges, either in person, by phone, or by a pop-up on an application or while surfing the web?

   _____

   _____

   _____

LAB 14-1

Discussing Security Fundamentals

Activity Time: 15 minutes

Scenario:

---

1. **Match the security concepts with the descriptions.**

   ___ Authentication
   ___ Encryption
   ___ Access control

   ___ Auditing

   a. Scrambling information so it cannot be read without a key
   b. Tracking system events
   c. Assigning rights and privileges on objects
   d. Identifying an individual

---

2. **Match the access control scheme with the description.**

   ___ Mandatory Access Control (MAC)
   ___ Discretionary Access Control (DAC)
   ___ Role-based Access Control (RBAC)

   a. Comparing a security designation with a clearance level
   b. Assigning users to roles that determine privileges
   c. Assigning customized access to objects for subjects

3. **How does multi-factor authentication enhance security?**

---

4. **True or False? A digital signature is an application of hashing encryption, because the signature is never transformed back to cleartext.**

   ___ True

   ___ False

---

5. **Which is stronger, symmetric or asymmetric encryption? Why?**

---

6. A user forwards an email with attachments to other users in the organization. The email states that a person was in dire need of help and to please forward the email to others immediately. It causes a virus to spread within the organization. What type of attack(s) did the attacker use?

7. Alicia needs a file from Jeff's computer to meet an important deadline, but he is at a three-day seminar in another city. She has spoken to Jeff, who offered to give her his password. Corporate security policies dictate that user passwords should never be shared. What could Alicia do to maintain security while meeting her deadline?

    a) Get Jeff's password during a phone call, and use it to retrieve the needed file.

    b) Contact the IT department to determine if a support technician can retrieve the file.

    c) Wait until Jeff returns, then get the file and complete the project.

8. For what are VPN and IPSec often used to implement security?

    a) Data removal

    b) Hardware disposal

    c) Data migration

    d) Wireless encryption

9. Betsy receives a call from Pietro, who says he has recently been hired as an IT technician, and has been assigned the task of updating user accounts. To implement this update for Betsy's account, he needs her username and password. What should Betsy do?

10. Which wireless security protocol is the strongest and most current?

    a) WEP

    b) WTLS

    c) WPA

    d) 802.11c

    e) 802.14

11. Your organization recently implemented wireless networking at a branch office. What suggestions would you make to ensure the security of the wireless network?

    a) Implement user authentication.

    b) Use a wireless security protocol that provides data encryption.

    c) Keep firmware and software, including anti-virus software, up to date.

    d) Keep the Wireless Access Point behind a firewall.

15 | Supporting Personal Computer Security

Activities included in this chapter:

- Exercise 15-1 Configuring Windows Firewall
- Exercise 15-2 Configuring NTFS Permissions
- Exercise 15-3 Using File Encryption
- Exercise 15-4 Maintaining and Troubleshooting Computer Security
- Lab 15-1 Configuring and Testing Local Security Policies

EXERCISE 15-1

Configuring Windows Firewall

Scenario:

A customer has asked you to configure Windows Firewall so that other users cannot use Remote Desktop to access his system from another computer on the network. He also wants to log dropped packets and successful connections.

There is a simulated version of this activity available on the CD-ROM that shipped with this course. You can run this simulation on any Windows computer to review the activity after class, or as an alternative to performing the activity as a group in class. The activity simulation can be launched either directly from the CD-ROM by clicking the Interactives link and navigating to the appropriate one, or from the installed data file location by opening the C:\ 085820Data\Simulations\Lesson#\Activity# folder and double-clicking the executable (.exe) file.

What You Do	How You Do It
1. **Disable the Remote Desktop exception.**	a. **Choose Start→Control Panel. Click Network And Internet Connections, and then click Windows Firewall.**
	b. On the General page, **verify that Windows Firewall is enabled. Click the Exceptions tab.**
	c. On the Exceptions page, **uncheck Remote Desktop.**
	d. To verify the ports you will close when you disable this exception, **click Edit.**

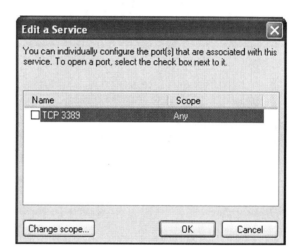

e. **Click OK.**

2. Configure logging.

a. **Click the Advanced tab.**

b. In the Security Logging section, **click Settings.**

c. **Check Log Dropped Packets and Log Successful Connections.**

d. **Verify that the log file will be created in the local C:\Windows folder and click OK twice.**

e. **Close the Network And Internet Connections window.**

Check Your Knowledge

1. What are Windows Security Policies and how can they help protect against attacks?

_____

_____

_____

2. How can biometric devices be used to enhance the security of a computer system or a facility?

_____

_____

_____

_____

_____

_____

3. Explain the importance of the Automatic Updates service in Windows.

_____

_____

_____

_____

EXERCISE 15-2

Configuring NTFS Permissions

Data Files:

\Security\Policy.txt

Before You Begin:

For this activity, you will need additional local user accounts.

1. Open Control Panel, and click User Accounts.

2. Click Create A New Account.

3. Name the new account User##, where ## is your computer number.

4. Select the Limited account type and create the account.

5. Create another Limited user account named OtherUser.

6. Close the User Accounts and Control Panel windows.

Conditions:

For this activity, you will need a copy of the Security folder from the student data file folder. The folder needs to be in the C:\ folder on your local hard drive. You might need to copy the folder before you begin the exercise. Be sure to remove the read-only attribute from the folder.

Scenario:

You administer the computers for your family-run, home-based business. The business computers are shared by everyone in the family, including your teenage children who work part-time for the business. You serve as the company's CEO and President.

As you're working, your spouse gives you a floppy disk containing a folder called Security, and asks you to copy it to your computer's hard drive. This folder contains confidential personnel policy files that you are developing for your company. You want to ensure that you can have access to these files without other company employees seeing their contents. You also want to account for the possibility that you might want to grant other users access to this folder in the future.

 There is a simulated version of this activity available on the CD-ROM that shipped with this course. You can run this simulation on any Windows computer to review the activity after class, or as an alternative to performing the activity as a group in class. The activity simulation can be launched either directly from the CD-ROM by clicking the Interactives link and navigating to the appropriate one, or from the installed data file location by opening the C:\ 085820Data\Simulations\Lesson#\Activity# folder and double-clicking the executable (.exe) file.

What You Do	**How You Do It**
1. **Create a local group and add the appropriate user account to it.**	a. **Choose Start, right-click My Computer and choose Manage.** b. **Expand Local Users And Groups and select the Groups folder.** c. **Choose Action→New Group.** d. In the Group Name text box, **type *Execs* and then click Add.** e. In the Enter The Object Names To Select text box, **type *User*##** where ## is your computer number. 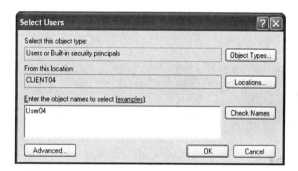 f. **Click Check Names and click OK.** g. **Click Create** to create the group and then **click Close.** h. **Close Computer Management.**
2. **Verify that the Administrators group has Full Control of the C:\Security folder. Grant the Execs group Full Control of the C:\Security folder.**	a. **Choose Start→My Computer.** b. **Double-click the C: drive.** c. **Select the Security folder and choose File→Properties.** d. **Click the Security tab.**

e. **Select the Administrators group. Verify that the Administrators group has Full Control.**

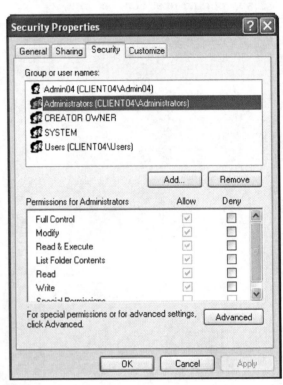

f. To add the Execs group to the permissions list, **click Add.**

g. In the Enter The Object Names To Select box, **type *execs***

h. **Click Check Names and then click OK.**

i. The Execs group appears in the permissions list. In the Group Or User Names list box, **select the Execs group.**

j. In the Permissions list, **check the Allow check box for the Full Control permission.**

k. **Click Apply.**

3. **Remove the Users group from the permissions list on the Security folder.**

a. In the Group Or User Names list box, **select the Users group.**

b. You can see from the gray check boxes that the Users group is inheriting some of its permissions from the C:\ folder. **Click Advanced.**

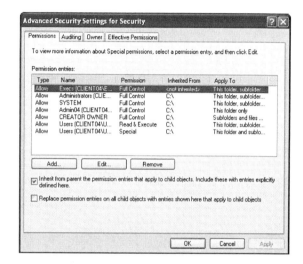

c. **Uncheck the Inherit From Parent The Permission Entries That Apply To Child Objects check box.**

d. To copy the permissions explicitly to the new folder so that you can edit them, **click Copy.**

e. **Click OK.**

f. In the Security Properties dialog box, **select the Users group.**

g. **Click Remove.**

h. **Click OK.**

4. Verify that the correct permissions are set on Policy.txt.

 a. **Open the Security folder.**

 b. **Select the Policy.txt file and choose File→Properties.**

 c. **Click the Security tab.**

 d. The Execs group appears in the Permissions list, but the Users group does not. Because you copied the file, it inherited permissions from its parent folder. **Click Cancel.**

 e. **Close the Security folder window.**

5. **Verify that authorized users have access to the Security folder and files and that unauthorized users do not.**

a. **Choose Start→Log Off.**

b. **Click Switch User.**

c. **Click OtherUser.**

d. **Choose Start→My Computer.**

e. **Open the C drive.**

f. If necessary, **click Show The Contents Of This Folder.**

g. **Double-click the Security folder.**

h. You should be denied access. To close the message box, **click OK.**

i. **Close the window.**

j. **Choose Start→Log Off.**

k. **Click Log Off.**

l. **Click Admin##** where ## is your computer number.

m. **Enter *!Pass1234***

Check Your Knowledge

1. You need to secure a folder on a shared drive on the network. How would you go about this?

_____

_____

_____

2. When configuring NTFS permissions, can you limit specific users from accessing a specific folder?

_____

_____

_____

_____

3. How can you limit a user group's access to a shared folder?

_____

_____

_____

4. How can you verify that your changes to NTFS permissions were correctly implemented?

_____

_____

_____

_____

_____

EXERCISE 15-3

Using File Encryption

Data Files:

\Encrypt\ClientNotes.rtf

Before You Begin:

For this activity, you will need a copy of the Encrypt folder from the student data file folder. The copy needs to be in the C:\ folder on your local hard drive. You might need to copy the folder before you begin the exercise. Be sure to remove the read-only attribute from the folder and its files. Grant the local Users group Full Control to the Encrypt folder and its contents.

Setup:

You have a local Admin## account, a User## account, and an OtherUser account.

Scenario:

You are the support person in a small, family-owned business that uses a workgroup-based Windows XP Professional network. One of your sales representatives is gathering confidential information about a prospective client, and wants to protect the information in the event that his laptop is ever lost or stolen when he is on the road.

There is a simulated version of this activity available on the CD-ROM that shipped with this course. You can run this simulation on any Windows computer to review the activity after class, or as an alternative to performing the activity as a group in class. The activity simulation can be launched either directly from the CD-ROM by clicking the Interactives link and navigating to the appropriate one, or from the installed data file location by opening the C:\ 085820Data\Simulations\Lesson#\Activity# folder and double-clicking the executable (.exe) file.

What You Do	How You Do It
1. **Encrypt the C:\Encrypt folder and its contents.**	a. **Choose Start→My Computer.**
	b. **Open the C: drive.**
	c. **Open the Encrypt folder.**
	d. To verify that you can open and read files in this folder, **open the ClientNotes.rtf file.**
	e. The file opens in WordPad. **Close WordPad.**
	f. **Click the Up button.**
	g. **Select the Encrypt folder and choose File→Properties.**
	h. On the General page, **click Advanced.**
	i. **Check Encrypt Contents To Secure Data.**

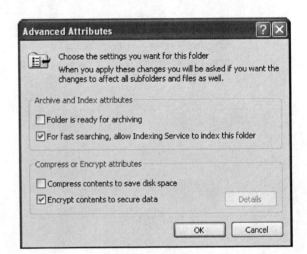

j. **Click OK twice.**

k. In the Confirm Attribute Changes dialog box, **verify that Apply Changes To This Folder, Subfolders And Files is selected.**

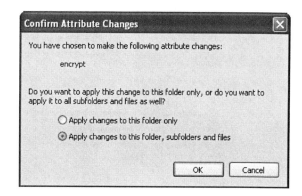

l. **Click OK.**

m. The encryption attribute is applied to all the files and subfolders. To de-select the Encrypt folder, **click the Windows folder.**

n. The name of the encrypted folder appears in a different color. **Close the window.**

2. **Test the encryption as another user.**

a. **Choose Start→Log Off.**

b. **Click Switch User.**

c. **Click User##** where ## is your computer number.

d. The Start menu opens. **Click My Computer.**

e. **Open the C drive.**

f. **Open the Encrypt folder.**

g. **Double-click ClientNotes.rtf.**

h. You should be denied access. To close the message box and WordPad, **click OK.**

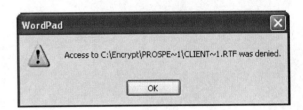

i. **Close the window.**

j. **Choose Start→Log Off.**

k. **Click Log Off.**

l. **Click Admin##** where ## is your computer number.

m. **Enter** *!Pass1234*

Check Your Knowledge

1. How can you protect the contents of a file from unauthorized access?

2. Which option do you enable to encrypt a file?

3. How can you verify if a file has been encrypted?

EXERCISE 15-4

Maintaining and Troubleshooting Computer Security

Scenario:

In this activity, you will discuss the appropriate computer security maintenance and troubleshooting steps to apply in a given situation.

---

1. What steps can you take to help ensure that physical access controls provide the appropriate security on an ongoing basis?

---

2. What are some important steps you can take to ensure that users contribute to the overall security of an organization?

---

3. Adam needs to access some files on his computer from a system in a testing lab. He shared the folder, but he cannot access the files from the lab location. What might be the problem and how would you correct it?

---

4. Becky is collaborating with a colleague in a partner company. They installed a shared application to exchange data and modify data, but they are unable to get the application to connect to each others' computers successfully. What might be the problem and how might you correct it?

---

5. Charles is complaining because he is locked out of the research lab. He is supposed to access the room using a hand scanner but the door is not opening. After verifying Charles' security authorizations and releasing the door so he can get to work, what should you do next?

---

6. **You are surprised when Denise, a marketing representative, visits your company with her laptop and is able to access your corporate network. What security issue might need attention in this situation?**

7. **Fran, a sales representative, has been promoted to management and will be travelling less than previously. Edgar has taken over Fran's territory and the company has re-deployed Fran's laptop to Edgar. Edgar has been denied access to Fran's client files. What might be the problem and how could you correct it?**

Check Your Knowledge

1. What are some common security issues that can affect data security?

2. What are some of the common issues that affect software-based firewalls?

3. What is one of the most common problems with encryption?

4. How can you improve the security of a wireless client and network?

LAB 15-1

Configuring and Testing Local Security Policies

Activity Time: 30 minutes

Scenario:

 You can find a suggested solution for this activity in the \Solutions\Configuring and Testing Local Security Policies.txt file in the data file location.

1. Set the password policies.

2. Set the account lockout policies.

3. Test the password policy by attempting to create a password that does not conform to the policies.

4. Use User Accounts in Control Panel or Local Users And Groups in Computer Management to set passwords for the Admin## and User## accounts that conform to the policy. Verify that you can log on with the new passwords.

5. Test the account lockout policy by deliberately locking out a user-level account.

6. As the Admin## user, use Local Users And Groups in Computer Management to unlock the locked user account. Verify that the User## account can log on.

Follow-up

In this course, you acquired the essential skills and information you will need to install, upgrade, repair, configure, troubleshoot, optimize, and perform preventative maintenance of basic personal computer hardware and operating systems. If you are getting ready for a career as an entry-level information technology (IT) professional or personal computer (PC) service technician, and if your job duties will include any type of PC service tasks or technical support for computer users, this course presented you with the background knowledge and skills you will require to be successful. Taking this course was also an important part of your preparation for the CompTIA A+ certification examinations, 2006 objectives (exam numbers 220-601, 220-602, 220-603, and 220-604), in order to become a CompTIA A+ Certified Professional.

Glossary

8008

Introduced by Intel in 1972, the 8008 was the first microprocessor to be supported by a high-level language compiler.

802.11a

A fast, secure, but relatively expensive protocol for wireless communication. The 802.11a protocol supports speeds up to 54 Mbps in the 5 GHz frequency.

802.11b

Also called WiFi, short for "wired fidelity," 802.11b is probably the most common and certainly the least expensive wireless network protocol used to transfer data among computers with wireless network cards or between a wireless computer or device and a wired LAN. The 802.11b protocol provides for an 11 Mbps transfer rate in the 2.4 GHz frequency.

802.11e

A draft wireless standard for home and business implementations that adds QoS and multimedia support features to 802.11a and 802.11b.

802.11g

A specification for wireless data throughput at the rate of up to 54 Mbps in the 2.4 GHz band that is a potential replacement for 802.11b.

802.11i

A complete wireless standard that adds strong encryption and authentication security to 802.11.

802.1x

An IEEE standard used to provide a port-based authentication mechanism for wireless communications using the 802.11a and 802.11b protocols.

abacus

An early calculating instrument that uses sliding beads in columns that are divided in two by a center bar.

access control

The process of determining and assigning privileges to various resources, objects, and data.

ACL

(Access Control List) In a DAC access control scheme, the list that is associated with each object, specifying the subjects that can access the object and their level of access.

adapter card

A printed circuit board that is installed in a slot on a system board to provide special functions for customizing or extending a computer's capabilities. Also referred to as expansion card, add-in, add-on, or board.

administrative shares

Hidden shares created by default on every Windows system. If administrative shares are deleted, by default, the system re-creates them when it restarts.

adware

Unwanted software loaded onto a system for the purposes of presenting commercial advertisements to the user.

AGP

(Accelerated Graphics Port) A bus architecture based on PCI and designed specifically to speed up 3D graphics.

algorithm

In encryption, the rule, system, or mechanism used to encrypt the data.

allocation unit

Same as cluster.

Analytical Engine

Charles Babbage's vision of a mechanical calculator that would follow programmed instructions to perform any mathematical operations. The engine could store results for use later, and look up values in tables and call on standard subroutines.

answer file

A text file that contains configuration settings that provide responses to prompts for information in the Windows Setup program.

antivirus software

An application that scans files for executable code that matches patterns known to be common to viruses, and monitors systems for activity associated with viruses.

APIPA

(Automatic Private IP Addressing) A service that configures a DHCP client computer with an IP address on the 169.254.0.0 network if no DHCP servers are available.

ASR

(Automated System Recovery) A process that uses backup data and the Windows XP Professional installation source files to rebuild a failed computer system.

ASR backup set

A backup set containing a complete copy of a Windows XP Professional installation.

ASR floppy disk

A floppy disk that enables a system to locate the ASR backup set.

asymmetric encryption

A two-way encryption scheme that uses paired private keys and public keys to perform encryption and decryption.

ATA

(Advanced Technology Attachment) The official ANSI term for IDE drives.

auditing

The process that tracks user and operating system activities by recording selected types of events in the security log of a server or a workstation.

authentication

A network security measure in which a computer user or some other network component proves its identity in order to gain access to network resources.

backup set

The unit of storage Windows Backup uses to store data on backup media.

bandwidth

A measurement of how much data a network medium is capable of carrying at any given time.

bank

Multiple rows of DRAM in a single system that can be accessed simultaneously.

base memory address

The memory address of any memory that might be on a device itself.

bindery

The flat-file, per-server network database system used in Novell NetWare prior to version 4.0.

biometrics

An automated method of recognizing a person based on a physiological or behavioral characteristic.

BIOS

(Basic Input/Output System) A set of instructions that is stored in Read Only Memory and that is used to start the most basic services of a computer system.

boot disk

In Windows, a floppy disk that you can use to start the system and bypass damaged or missing Windows startup files.

BPL

(Broadband over Power Lines) A new and somewhat controversial technology that transmits network signals over an existing electrical power line grid.

broadband communications

A category of network transmission technologies that provide high throughput by splitting communications into multiple channels transmitted simultaneously over the network media.

bus

In a computer system, a collection of wires that connect components and the rules that describe how data should be transferred through the connection. They provide a pathway for data transfer.

bus master

A technology that takes control of the bus away from the CPU to transfer data directly to RAM or other devices.

cable tester

An electrical instrument that verifies if a signal is present on a cable. Also called a media tester.

cable transmissions

A WAN connectivity technology that uses a cable television connection and a specialized interface device known as a cable modem to provide high-speed Internet access to homes and small businesses.

cache memory

A type of memory that services the CPU. Level 1 (L1) cache is built into the CPU chip. Level 2 cache (L2) feeds the L1 cache. L2 can be built into the CPU chip, reside on a separate chip, or be a separate bank of chips on the system board. If L2 is built into the CPU, then level 3 cache (L3) can be present on the system board.

CardBus

A bus mastering technology used on PC Cards.

CCD array

(charge-coupled device array) Converts light reflections into electrical charges.

cellular WAN

A WAN technology that uses cellular radio signals to transmit network data over the cellular telephone system.

centralized network

A network in which a central host computer controls all network communication and performs the data processing and storage on behalf of network clients.

chip creep

The phenomenon of vibrations and movements causing components such as CPUs to become loosened in their connections.

chipset

The set of chips on the system board that support the CPU and other basic functions.

Class A addresses

A block of IP addresses from 1.0.0.0 to 127.255.255.255 that provides the largest number of nodes (16,777,214) and the smallest number of networks (126).

Class B addresses

A block of IP addresses from 128.0.0.0 to 191.255.255.255 that provides a good balance between the number of networks and the number of nodes per network—16,382 networks of 65,534 nodes each.

Class C addresses

A block of IP addresses from 192.0.0.0 to 223.255.255.255 that provides the largest number of networks (2,097,150) and the smallest number of nodes per network (254).

Class D addresses

A block of IP addresses from 224.0.0.0 to 239.255.255.255 used to support multicast sessions.

Class E addresses

A block of IP addresses from 240.0.0.0 to 255.255.255.255 used for research and experimentation purposes.

client

A computer whose primary role is to make use of the services and resources of other computers.

client/server network

A network in which some computers act as servers to provide special services on behalf of other client computers.

cluster

A group of sectors that is the smallest unit of storage allotted on a given drive.

CMOS RAM

(Complementary Metal Oxide Semiconductor) Special memory that has its own battery to help it keep track of its data even when the power is turned off, and that stores information about the computer setup that the system BIOS refers to each time the computer starts.

coax

Pronounced "CO-ax," this term is a common abbreviation for coaxial cable.

coaxial cable

A type of copper cable that features a central conductor surrounded by braided or foil shielding. A dialectric insulator separates the conductor and shield and the entire package is wrapped in an insulating layer called a jacket. The data signal is transmitted over the central conductor. The outer shielding serves to reduce electromagnetic interference.

Computer case

The encloser that holds all of the components of the computer.

computer image

A file containing a sector-by-sector replica of a computer's hard disk that can be replicated onto another computer's hard disk. Also called a clone image or ghost image.

computer network

A group of computers that are connected together to communicate and share resources.

control set

A registry key that contains a complete description of system configuration.

cooling system

A system unit component that prevents damage to computer parts by dissipating the heat generated inside a computer chassis.

corona

An assembly within a laser printer that contains a wire (the corona wire), which is responsible for charging the paper.

CPU

(central processing unit) The main chip on the system board, the CPU performs software instructions and mathematical and logical equations. Also referred to as the microprocessor or processor.

DAC

(Discretionary Access Control) An access control method in which access is controlled based on a user's identity and the properties of objects are configured to allow or deny access to user identities.

data access policy

A group of policy provisions or software policy settings that control who can access computer systems and the data they store.

data backup

A system-maintenance task that enables you to store copies of critical files and folders on another medium for safekeeping.

data bus

The connection between the CPU, memory, and peripheral devices.

data restoration

A system recovery task that enables you to access the backed-up data.

daughter board

Any circuit board that plugs into another.

Deep Sleep

Drastically reduced power mode entered into after certain conditions (such as prolonged inactivity) have been met.

definition

A code pattern that identifies a virus. Also called a signature.

device driver

Software that enables the operating system and a peripheral device to communicate with each other. Often referred to as driver software or driver.

DHCP

(Dynamic Host Configuration Protocol) A network service that provides automatic assignment of IP addresses and other TCP/IP configuration information.

dial-up connections

Network connections that use telecommunications media, such as modems, existing phone lines, and existing long-distance carrier services to provide low-cost, low-bandwidth WAN connectivity and remote network access.

Diffie-Hellman

A cryptographic protocol that provides for secure key exchange.

digital signature

A piece of encrypted data attached to a file to verify the integrity of the file.

diode

An electronic component that acts like a one-way valve. Diodes are often used to change Alternating Current (AC) to Direct Current (DC), as temperature or light sensors, and as light emitters.

DIP switch

(Dual Inline Package) Switches on a card used to configure hardware settings. These are usually rocker switches (like light switches) to turn on or off.

direct thermal printer

A thermal printer that uses heated pins to form images directly onto specially-coated thermal paper.

directory

A component in a file system hierarchy that provides a container to organize files and other directories (folders).

directory service

On a network, a centralized database that includes objects such as servers, clients, computers, user names, and passwords, and provides centralized administration and authentication.

disk cloning

The process of copying the contents of one hard disk to another.

disk partition

An isolated section of a disk that functions like a separate physical drive.

display device

A personal computer component that enables users to view the text and graphical data associated with a computer program.

DMA

(Direct Memory Access) Specialized circuitry or a dedicated microprocessor that transfers data from adapters to memory without using the CPU.

docking solution

Any device that that simplifies the task of connecting and disconnecting external peripherals from the portable system.

domain

A Microsoft network model that an administrator implements by grouping computers together for the purpose of sharing a centralized user account database. Sharing this user account database enables users to use these accounts to log on at any computer in the domain.

domain controller

A server that stores the user account database for the domain and is responsible for authenticating users when they log on to the domain.

dongle

An adapter that plugs into a PC Card and has a connector on the other end for plugging in a phone cord or network cable.

dot-matrix printer

An impact printer that forms images out of dots on paper by using a set of pins to strike an inked ribbon.

drive image

A computer file containing the complete contents and structure of a data-storage medium or device.

drive rails

Metal adapters you screw onto a 3.5" hard drive in order to install it into a 5.25" drive bay.

DSL

(Digital Subscriber Line) A broadband Internet connection method that transmits digital signal over existing phone lines.

dual-core processor

A multi-core processor with two separate processors.

dump file

The file that stores the contents of a memory dump.

dye sublimation printer

Same as thermal dye transfer printer.

ECC

(Error Correction Code) An error correction method that uses several bits for error-checking.

eDirectory

Novell's standards-based, enterprise-level directory service; an evolution of the earlier NDS directory.

EDSAC

(Electronic Delay Storage Automatic Computer) A well-engineered machine built by Maurice Wilkes and colleagues at the University of Cambridge Mathematics Lab in 1949 and was a productive tool for mathematicians.

EDVAC

(Electronic Discrete Variable Automatic Computer) The first computer to use stored programs.

EISA bus

(Extended Industry Standard Architecture bus) A PC bus standard that extends the 16-bit ISA bus (AT bus) to 32 bits and provides bus mastering.

electrical interference

A general term for unwanted signals on the network media that can interfere with network transmissions.

electrical noise

Same as electrical interference.

Elgamal

A public-key encryption algorithm developed by Taher Elgamal.

encryption

A network security measure in which information is encoded or scrambled prior to transmission so that it cannot be read unless the recipient knows the decoding mechanism, or key.

ENIAC

(Electronic Numerical Integrator And Computer) Developed for the U.S. Army by J. Presper Eckert and John Mauchly at the University of Pennsylvania in Philadelphia. ENIAC was programmed by plugging in cords and setting thousands of switches to direct how 18,000 vacuum tubes would perform 5,000 calculations per second.

EP drum

(Electrostatic Photographic drum) The component in a laser printer that carries the electrical charge to attract toner and then to transfer the toner to the paper.

ERD

(emergency repair disk) A disk that contains information about the current configuration of the operating system and that can be used to repair problems with the operating system.

ESD

(Electrostatic discharge) The phenomenon that occurs when electrons rush from one body with a static electrical charge to another with an unequal charge, following the path of least resistance.

FC-AL

(Fibre Channel-Arbitrated Loop) A Fibre Channel implementation that can connect up to 127 nodes without using a switch. All devices share the bandwidth, and only two can communicate with each other at the same time, with each node repeating the data to its adjacent node.

FDD

(floppy disk drive) A personal computer storage device that reads data from and writes data to removable disks made of flexible, Mylar plastic covered with a magnetic coating, and enclosed in a stiff, protective, plastic case.

fiber optic cable

A type of cable in which one or more glass or plastic strands, plus additional fiber strands or wraps, are surrounded by a protective outer jacket. Light pulses carry the signal through fiber optic cable.

Fibre Channel

A network technology that supports data transfers at speeds from 1 Gb/second up to 4 Gb/second.

firewall

A software program or hardware device that protects networks from unauthorized data by blocking unsolicited traffic.

FireWire connection

A high-speed serial bus developed by Apple and Texas Instruments that allows for the connection of up to 63 devices. Used interchangeably with IEEE 1394.

firmware

Software stored in memory chips that retains data whether or not power to the computer is on.

flashing

Updating firmware.

folder

Same as directory.

form factor

The size and shape of a given component. Often used in terms of motherboard and drive characteristics.

formed-character printer

Any type of impact printer that functions like a typewriter, by pressing preformed characters against the ink ribbon to deposit the ink on the page.

FTP

(File Transfer Protocol) A protocol used to upload files to or download files from an FTP file server.

Fuel Cell

A battery technology that combines hydrogen and oxygen to generate an electric current.

full duplex

A mode of communication that permits two-way transmission. It can both send and receive at the same time.

fusing assembly

A component in a laser printer that uses two rollers to heat toner particles, melting them into the paper.

GDI

(Graphics Device Interface) The spooler component that provides the communications interface between an application and the Windows printing system.

grayware

A general classification for any unwanted software that produces harmful or annoying effects.

half duplex

A mode of communication that permits two-way transmission, but in only one direction at a time.

hash

The value that results from hashing encryption. Same as hash value and message digest.

hash value

Same as hash.

hashing encryption

One-way encryption that transforms cleartext into a coded form that is never decrypted.

HDD

(hard disk drive) A personal computer storage device that uses fixed media and magnetic data storage.

high-level formatting

An operating system function that builds file systems on drives and partitions.

hijacking

An attack in which an attacker could takes over a valid user's session on a wireless network.

hoax

Any message containing incorrect or misleading information that is disseminated to multiple users through unofficial channels.

host

In a centralized network, the computer that controls network functions. In a TCP/IP network, any computer.

hot swapping

Replacing a device without needing to power down the PC during removal of the old device or installation of the new device. Also referred to as hot plug or hot insertion.

HTML

(HyperText Markup Language) The authoring language used to create documents on the web.

HTTP

(HyperText Transfer Protocol) A protocol that defines the interaction between a web server and a browser.

HTTPS

(HyperText Transfer Protocol Secure) A secure version of HTTP that supports e-commerce by providing a secure connection between web browser and server.

HVD

(High-voltage differential) A SCSI signaling scheme that uses two wires, one for data and one for the inverse of data. HVD devices use high voltage and cannot be used on a single-ended SCSI chain.

I/O address

A range of memory, usually in the lowest portions of memory (conventional memory), that is used for communications between the processor and the adapter. Each adapter must have its own unique, non-overlapping I/O address space.

IEEE

(Institute of Electrical and Electronic Engineers) Pronounced "I-triple-E." An organization of scientists, engineers, and students of electronics and related fields whose technical and standards committees develop, publish, and revise computing and telecommunications standards.

IMAP4

(Internet Mail Access Protocol) A protocol used to retrieve email messages and folders from a mail server.

impact printer

Any type of printer that strikes a component directly against the paper or ink to create characters on the paper.

incident report

A record of any instance where a person is injured or computer equipment is damaged due to environmental issues. Also, a record of accidents involving hazardous materials, such as chemical spills, that could have an impact on the environment itself.

INF file

An information file is a file with a .inf extension that is shipped with a device that provides the information necessary for the operating system to install the device, such as the name of the device's driver file.

infrared

A form of wireless connection in which signals are sent via pulses of infrared light.

ink dispersion printer

Same as inkjet printer.

inkjet printer

A printer that forms images by spraying ink on the paper.

input device

A personal computer component that enables users to enter data or instructions into a computer.

instruction set

The collection of commands used by a CPU to perform calculations and other computing operations.

integrated circuit

An electronic component consisting of several transistors and resistors, connected together on a semiconductor chip.

interrupt

A signal sent over an IRQ that informs the processor that the device needs its attention.

IP address

A 32-bit binary number assigned to a computer on a TCP/IP network.

ipconfig

A Windows troubleshooting tool used to verify the configuration of TCP/IP and to release or renew DHCP IP address leases.

IPSec

(Internet Protocol security) A set of open, non-proprietary standards that you can use to secure data as it travels across the network or the Internet through data authentication and encryption.

IPX/SPX

(Internetwork Packet Exchange/Sequenced Packet Exchange) A proprietary routable network protocol developed by Novell for use in versions 3 and 4 of the Novell NetWare network operating system.

IrDA

(Infrared Data Association) The standards organization responsible for defining the communication protocol standards for wireless PANs that communicate using infrared light.

IRQ

(Interrupt Request line) A hardware line connected to a controller chip and assigned to a device. When the device needs to request the attention of the computer processor, it sends a signal over the IRQ line.

ISA bus

(Industry Standard Architecture bus) An expansion bus commonly used in PCs.

iSCSI

(Internet SCSI) A protocol that serializes SCSI commands so that they can be transferred over a TCP/IP network.

ISDN

(Integrated Services Digital Network) A digital transmission technology that carries both voice and data.

ISP

(Internet Service Provider) A company that provides access to the Internet.

jumper

Pins and connectors used to configure hardware settings. You physically connect or disconnect a circuit by adding or removing a jumper block, which is a small rectangular connector, from a pair of pins attached to the system board or add-on card.

key

In an encryption scheme, the piece of information required to encode or decode the encrypted data.

LAN

(local area network) A self-contained network that spans a small area, such as a single building, floor, or room.

laptop computer

A complete computer system that is small, lightweight, and portable.

laser printer

A type of printer that forms high-quality images on one page of paper at a time, by using a laser beam, toner, and an electrophotographic drum.

LDAP

(Lightweight Directory Access Protocol) A communications protocol that defines how a client can access information, perform operations, and share directory data on a directory server.

LED

(Light Emitting Diode) An indicator light on network adapters and on some other types of network equipment.

Li-Ion

Portable computer lithium battery with a long life.

Linux

An open-standards UNIX derivative originally developed and released by a Finnish computer science student named Linus Torvalds.

Linux distribution

A complete Linux implementation, including kernel, shell, applications, and utilities, that is packaged, distributed, and supported by a software vendor.

Lithium Polymer

Portable computer battery using a jelly-like material.

Local Area Connection Status

A Windows troubleshooting tool used to verify that the LAN is connected to the network and able to send and receive data.

local printer

A logical printer that is managed by the local computer, where the print device is generally directly attached.

lockup error

An error condition that causes the system or an application to stop responding to user input.

logic bomb

A piece of code that sits dormant on a user's computer until it's triggered by a specific event, such as a specific date. Once the code is triggered, the logic bomb "detonates," erasing and corrupting data on the user's computer.

loopback plug

A special connector used for diagnosing network transmission problems that redirects electrical signals back to the transmitting system.

low-level formatting

The process of writing track and sector markings on a disk.

LVD

(Low-voltage differential) A SCSI signaling technique that uses two wires, one for data and one for the inverse of data. LVD devices use a low voltage and can be used on a single-ended SCSI chain.

MAC

(Mandatory Access Control) An access control method in which objects (files and other resources) are assigned security labels of varying levels, depending on the object's sensitivity, and then matched to a user's clearance level.

MAC address

(Media Access Control address) Same as the physical address.

magnetic core memory

Memory that stores binary data (0 or 1) in the orientation of magnetic charges in ferrite cores about one-sixteenth-inch in diameter.

malicious software

Any unwanted software that has the potential to damage a system or create a nuisance condition.

Mark I

A programmable, electromechanical calculator that combined 78 adding machines to perform three calculations per second. It was designed by Howard Aiken, built by IBM, and installed at Harvard in 1944.

MD5

(Message Digest 5) This hash algorithm, based on RFC 1321, produces a 128-bit hash value and is used in IPSec policies for data authentication.

media tester

See cable tester.

memory

A personal computer component that describes the internal storage areas of the computer.

memory dump

The process of writing the contents of system memory at the time of a stop error to a file on the hard disk prior to system shutdown.

memory module

A system unit component that holds a group of memory chips that act as a single memory chip.

message digest

A hash value generated from an electronic message.

MiB

(mebibyte) A contraction of the terms mega binary byte that represents a unit of computer storage where 1 MiB = 2^20 bytes, or 1,048,576 bytes. The mebibyte is closely related to the megabyte, which is typically viewed as 1,000,000 bytes. Although the terms MiB and MB are often used as synonyms, mistaking the two can occasionally lead to problems when referring to electronic equipment.

Micro Channel Architecture bus

A proprietary 32-bit bus from IBM that was used in PS/2, RS/6000, and certain ES/9370 models.

microDIMM

(Micro Dual Inline Memory Module) A memory module standard used in small, sub-compact notebooks.

microprocessor

A complete central processing unit on a single chip, the microprocessor controls the operation of all the other computer components.

mixed mode network

A network that displays characteristics of more than one of the three standard network models.

motherboard

Same as system board.

MSDS

(Material Safety Data Sheet) A technical bulletin designed to give users and emergency personnel information about the proper procedures of storage and handling of a hazardous substance.

multi-core processor

A central processing unit that consists of two (or more) processors combined into a single package. A multi-core processor enables the computers to process multiple threads simultaneously without requiring you to install two separate and distinct CPUs. Dual-core processors are a type of multi-core processor.

multi-factor authentication

Any authentication scheme that requires validation of at least two of the possible authentication factors.

multi-function device

A piece of office equipment that performs the functions of a number of other specialized devices.

multimedia device

A computer peripheral or internal component that transfers sound or images to or from a personal computer.

multimeter

An electronic instrument used to measure voltage, current, and resistance.

Napier's Bones

A set of rectangular rods with numbers etched on them that let users do multiplication by adding the numbers on properly positioned rods. Precursor of the slide rule.

NAS

(Network-Attached Storage) A storage device that you connect to a network and users directly access (instead of going through a server as with SANs). NAS devices use their own software to provide users with access to their data.

NDS

(Novell Directory Services) Novell's original X.500-based directory service.

NetBEUI

(NetBIOS Extended User Interface) A fast, simple protocol developed by Microsoft and IBM for implementation on small networks.

NetBIOS

(Network Basic Input/Output System) A specification that enables applications and services to use different network protocols to communicate with each other when they are running on different systems within the network. NetBIOS naming and communications were heavily used in many Microsoft operating systems and Microsoft computers still support NetBIOS naming.

network address

An identifier, typically a number, that is assigned to a network computer for a specific network protocol.

network client

A software component that enables a computer to access a shared resource on another computer.

network printer

A logical printer that represents a connection to a shared print device managed by a network print server.

network protocol

Software that provides the rules by which network operations are conducted.

network-connnected printers

A print device with a network adapter card that connects directly to a network cable.

NiCad

Portable computer battery made of nickel and cadmium with a three to four hour life.

NiMH

Environmentally friendly battery for portable computers.

node

A generalized term for any network device with its own address.

nslookup

A Windows troubleshooting tool used to verify that the computer can connect to a DNS server and successfully find an IP address for a given computer name.

on-die

Integrated directly into a semiconductor chip.

online UPS

A UPS that supplies power from a battery at all times. The battery is charged from the regular electrical supply.

open standards

Any type of software-development standards that are arrived at cooperatively and are not owned or maintained by any particular organization or commercial enterprise.

optical disk

A personal computer storage device that stores data optically, rather than magnetically.

page

A section of memory addresses in which a unit of data can be stored.

page fault

An interrupt generated when an application requests data that is no longer present in its virtual memory location.

pagefile

In a virtual-memory system, the section of the hard disk used to store memory contents that have been swapped out of physical RAM. In Windows XP Professional, the pagefile is called Pagefile.sys.

paging

See swapping.

Paillier cryptosystem

An asymmetric encryption algorithm developed by Pascal Paillier.

PAN

(personal area network) A network of devices used by a single individual.

parallel connection

A personal computer connection type that transfers data eight bits at a time over eight wires and is often used for a printer.

parity

An error correction method for electronic communications.

Pascaline machine

A calculating machine that could add and subtract, developed in 1642 by Blaise Pascal.

PATA connection

(Parallel Advanced Technology Attachment) A personal computer connection that provides a parallel data channel from a disk controller to the disk drives. Also referred to as IDE, EIDE, or ATA.

patches

Targeted operating system updates that Microsoft and other system vendors release on an as-needed basis to provide enhancements to the operating system or to address security or performance issues.

PC

(Personal Computers) Stand-alone, single-user desktop, or smaller, computers that can function independently. PC used to refer to any personal computer, but now refers to personal computers that follow the original design by IBM, use Intel or compatible chips, and usually have some version of Windows as an operating system. PCs are sometimes called IBM compatibles.

PC Card

The credit-card-sized devices that are used in portable computers instead of desktop-sized expansion cards.

PCI bus

(Peripheral Component Interconnect bus) A peripheral bus commonly used in PCs that provides a high-speed data path between the CPU and peripheral devices.

PCI Express

A video adapter bus that is based on the PCI computer bus. PCIe supports significantly enhanced performance over that of AGP.

PCMCIA

(Personal Computer Memory Card International Association) An association of organizations that establishes standards for PC Cards.

peer-to-peer network

A network in which resource sharing, processing, and communications control are completely decentralized.

permissions

Security settings that control access to individual objects, such as files.

personal computer connection

The collection of hardware components that enables the computer to communicate with internal or external devices.

PGP

(Pretty Good Privacy) A method of securing emails created to prevent attackers from intercepting and manipulating email and attachments by encrypting and digitally signing the contents of the email using public key cryptography.

phishing

A type of email-based social engineering attack, in which the attacker sends email from a spoofed source, such as a bank, to try to elicit private information from the victim.

Physical Access Controls

Measures that restrict access to specific physical areas.

physical address

For network adapter cards, a globally unique hexadecimal number burned into every adapter by the manufacturer.

ping

A Windows troubleshooting tool used to test communications between two TCP/IP-based hosts.

plenum

An air handling space, including ducts and other parts of the HVAC system in a building.

plenum cable

A grade of cable that does not give off noxious or poisonous gases when burned. Unlike PVC cable, plenum cable can be run through the plenum and firebreak walls.

POP3

(Post Office Protocol version 3) A protocol used to retrieve email from a mailbox on the mail server.

port

A hardware connection interface on a personal computer that enables devices to be connected to the computer.

port monitor

The spooler component that physically transfers the print job to the print device.

portable computing device

Any one of a number of devices with some computing capability that can easily be moved from one location to another.

POST

(Power-On Self Test) A built-in diagnostic program that is run every time a personal computer starts up.

POTS

(Plain Old Telephone Service) Another name for traditional local and long distance telephone networks.

power supply

An internal computer component that converts AC power from an electrical outlet to the DC power needed by system components.

print driver

Software that manages the communication between computer programs and specific printers or plotters.

print processor

The spooler component that readies a print job for the printer.

print provider

The spooler component that communicates between the computer and the print device.

print queue

A list of jobs waiting to print.

print router

The spooler component that determines the correct print provider.

print server

A computer somewhere on the network with a local printer that has been shared for network clients to use.

print spooler

A Windows® system component that manages the printing process.

printer

An output device that produces text and images from electronic content onto physical media such as paper or transparency film.

proprietary development

Software development or standards that are owned, maintained, or copyrighted by a particular organization, and cannot be used freely without purchase or permission.

PSTN

(Public Switched Telephone Network) A term for traditional local and long distance telephone networks.

public-key encryption

The same as asymmetric encryption.

PVC

(Polyvinyl chloride) A flexible rubber-like plastic used to surround some twisted pair cabling. It is flexible and inexpensive, but gives off noxious or poisonous gases when burned.

Quick Start

Power-saving mode supported by many Intel Mobile processors.

RAID

(Redundant Array of Independent Disks) An arrangement of multiple disk drives and a sophisticated controller that provides higher performance or reliability, or both, than a single disk drive.

RAM chip

An integrated circuit that acts as the computer's primary temporary storage place for data. RAM stands for Random Access Memory.

RBAC

(Role-based Access Control) An access control method in which users are assigned to roles, and network objects are configured to allow access only to specific roles. Roles are created independently of user accounts.

Recovery Console

A minimal version of Windows XP Professional that provides a command-line interface to a Windows XP Professional installation.

registry

The central configuration database where Windows stores and retrieves startup settings, hardware and software configuration information, and information for local user accounts.

remanence

Magnetic signals that linger on storage media after erasure or deletion.

rendering

Creating a print job in printer language from the print job submitted by an application.

resistor

An electronic component that resists the flow of electric current in an electronic circuit.

restore point

A collection of information about changes to core system components, created and stored by the System Restore service.

right

A security mechanism that enables a user to perform a system-wide action, such as shutting down the computer.

riser card

A board that is plugged into the system board and provides additional slots for adapter cards.

rotation method

The schedule that determines how many backup tapes or other media sets are needed, and the sequence in which they are used and reused.

RSA

The first successful algorithm to be designed for public-key encryption. It is named for its designers, Rivest, Shamir, and Adelman.

S/MIME

(Secure Multipurpose Internet Mail Extensions) S/MIME prevents attackers from intercepting and manipulating email and attachments by encrypting and digitally signing the contents of the email using public key cryptography.

Safe Mode

A system startup method that loads only a minimal set of drivers and services.

SAM

(Sequential Access Memory) Used for memory areas where data can be stored in sequential order, such as memory buffers.

SAN

(Storage Area Network) A Fibre Channel network that enables a server to access a number of storage devices such as drive arrays and tape libraries.

SAS

(Serial Attached SCSI) A serial version of the SCSI interface. SAS is a point-to-point architecture that uses a disk controller with four or more channels operating simultaneously. SAS also supports serial ATA (SATA) drives, which can be mixed with SAS drives in a variety of configurations.

scanner

A device that creates a two-dimensional digitized image of a physical object.

SCSI

(Small Computer System Interface) A older personal computer connection standard hat provides high-performance data transfer between the SCSI device and the other components of the computer. Pronounced scuzzy.

sector

Individual storage areas on a formatted disk.

security policy

A formalized statement that defines how security will be implemented within a particular organization.

separator page

A page of printer code that can be sent ahead of a print job.

separator page processor

The spooler component that inserts the separator page.

Serial ATA connection

A personal computer connection that provides a serial data channel between the drive controller and the disk drives.

serial connection

A personal computer connection that transfers data one bit at a time over a single wire and is often used for an external modem.

server

A computer that provides services and resources on the network.

service

A background process in Windows that runs independently of a user logon and performs a specific operation.

Service Packs

Comprehensive software updates that generally include all prior patches and updates, but which can also include important new features and functions.

SHA

(Secure Hash Algorithm) This hash algorithm is modeled after MD5 and is considered the stronger of the two because it produces a 160-bit hash value.

share

A network resource, such as a disk, folder, or printer, that is available to other computer users on the network.

shared-key encryption

The same as symmetric encryption.

signature

A code pattern that identifies a virus. Also called a definition.

signed device driver

A driver that has been tested and verified for a particular operating system, and has a piece of digital signature attached to it by a signing authority.

site survey

An analysis technique that determines the coverage area of a wireless network, identifies any sources of interference, and establishes other characteristics of the coverage area.

smart card

A device similar to a credit card that can store authentication information, such as a user's private key, on an embedded microchip.

SMTP

(Simple Mail Transfer Protocol) A communications protocol used to send email from a client to a server or between servers.

social engineering attack

A type of attack where the goal is to obtain sensitive data, including user names and passwords, from network users through deception and trickery.

SODIMM

(Small Outline Dual Inline Memory Module) A memory module standard used in some notebook and iMac systems.

software diagnostic tool

A computer repair tool that contains programs that test hardware and software components. Also referred to as utility.

soldered

A means of securing electronic components to a circuit board by using a combination of lead, tin, and silver (solder) and a tool called a soldering iron.

solid ink printer

A type of printer that uses ink from melted solid-ink sticks.

solid state storage

A personal computer storage device that stores data in special types of memory instead of on disks or tape.

spam

Can refer either to frequent and repetitive postings in electronic bulletin boards, or more commonly to unsolicited or distasteful commercial email from anonymous sources.

SpeedStep

Technology that enables two different performance modes, Maximized Performance Mode and Battery Optimized Mode. In Maximized Performance Mode, the processor runs at its highest speed and normal internal voltage. In Battery Optimized Mode, the processor runs at a reduced speed and a reduced internal voltage.

spooling

Writing a print job from memory to disk.

spyware

Unwanted software that collects personal user data from a system and transmits it to a third party.

SSA

(Serial Storage Architecture) A fault-tolerant peripheral interface that transfers data at 80 and 160 MB/sec. SSA uses SCSI commands, allowing existing software to drive SSA peripherals such as disk drives. SSA uses a ring architecture that supports up to 128 devices; if one fails, the remaining devices continue to run. SSA distances are 25 meters over copper and 2.4 kilometers over fiber. SSA was designed to provide an alternative to Fibre Channel, but has not been as widely used.

SSL

(Secure Sockets Layer) A security protocol that uses certificates for authentication and encryption to protect web communication.

static electricity

The building up of a stationary electrical charge on any object.

Stepped Reckoner

A mechanical calculator developed by Gottfried von Leibniz that improved Pascal's design to include multiplication and division.

stop error

A system error severe enough to stop all processes and shut the system down without warning. Often referred to as "blue-screen errors" because they generate an error message screen with a blue background.

storage device

A computer component that enables users to save data for reuse at a later time, even after the personal computer is shut down and restarted.

subnet mask

A 32-bit number that is assigned to each host to divide the 32-bit binary IP address into network and node portions.

SUPS

(standby UPS) An SUPS is a UPS that supplies power from a battery when power problems are detected. Also referred to as a Standby Power Supply (SPS).

swapping

In a virtual memory system, the process of moving data back and forth from physical RAM to the pagefile. Also called paging.

symmetric encryption

A two-way encryption scheme in which encryption and decryption are both performed by the same key.

system BIOS

The Basic Input/Output System that sets the computer's configuration and environment when the system is powered on.

system board

The main circuit board in a computer that acts as the backbone for the entire computer system. Also referred to as motherboard.

system bus

The primary communication pathway between a CPU and other parts of the chipset. The system bus enables data transfer between the CPU, BIOS, memory, and the other buses in the computer. Also referred to as frontside bus or local bus.

System State

A subset of system components, including the Registry, that is backed up as a unit.

system unit

A personal computer component that houses other devices necessary for the computer to function, including the chassis, power supply, cooling device, system board, microprocessor, memory chips, disk drives, adapter cards, and ports for connecting external devices. Often referred to as a box, main unit, or base unit.

tape drive

A personal computer storage device that stores data magnetically on a removable tape.

TCP/IP

(Transmission Control Protocol/Internet Protocol) A nonproprietary, routable network protocol suite that enables computers to communicate over a network, including the Internet.

Telnet

A terminal emulation protocol that enables a user at one site to simulate a session on a remote host.

terminal

A client node on a centralized network, with few or no local computing resources of its own.

termination

Adding a resistor to the end of a coax network segment to prevent reflections that would interfere with the proper reception of network signals.

thermal dye transfer printer

A sophisticated type of color printer that uses heat to diffuse dye from color ribbons onto special paper or transparency blanks to produce continuous-tone output similar in quality to a photographic print. Also called dye sublimation printer.

thermal printer

Any printer that uses heat to create the image on the paper with dye or ink from ribbons or with heated pins.

thermal wax transfer printer

Thermal printer that uses a thermal printhead to melt wax-based ink from a transfer ribbon onto the paper.

throughput

A measurement of how much data can actually pass through the channel in a given time period.

toner

An electrically charged dry ink substance used in laser printers.

tracert

A Windows troubleshooting tool used to determine the route that the computer uses to send a packet to its destination. If tracert is unsuccessful, you can use the results generated to determine at what point communications are failing.

traces

Wires soldered on to the motherboard to provide communication paths for a bus on the system.

transistor

A device containing semiconductor material that can amplify a signal or open and close a circuit. In computers, transistors function as an electronic switch.

triboelectric generation

Using friction to create a static charge.

Trojan horse

Malicious code that masquerades as a harmless file. When a user executes it, thinking it's a harmless application, it destroys and corrupts data on the user's hard drive.

tunneling

A data-transport technique in which a data packet is transferred inside the frame or packet of another protocol, enabling the infrastructure of one network to be used to travel to another network.

twisted pair

A type of cable in which multiple insulated conductors are twisted around each other and clad in a protective and insulating outer jacket.

unattended installation

A Windows installation method that is automated to require limited or no user intervention.

UNIVAC

The Universal Automatic Computer was completed in 1951 by Eckert and Mauchly for the U.S. Bureau of the Census. It was the first commercial computer in the United States and could handle both numerical and alphabetical information.

UNIX

A family of operating systems originally developed at Bell Laboratories and characterized by portability, multiuser support, and built-in multitasking and networking functions.

UPS

(Uninterruptible Power Supply) A battery-operated device that is intended to save computer components from damage due to power problems such as power failures, spikes, and sags.

USB

(Universal Serial Bus) A hardware interface standard designed to provide connections for numerous peripherals.

USB connection

A personal computer connection that enables you to connect multiple peripherals to a single port with high performance and minimal device configuration.

user profile

A user-specific selection of settings and files found on Windows systems in the %systemroot%\ Documents and Settings folder.

vacuum tube

A sealed glass or metal container that controls a flow of electrons through a vacuum.

virtual memory

The ability of the computer system to use a portion of the hard disk as if it were physical RAM.

virus

A sample of code that spreads from one computer to another by attaching itself to other files. The code in a virus corrupts and erases files on a user's computer, including executable files, when the file to which it was attached is opened or executed. The term is often used as an umbrella term to refer to many types of malicious software.

VL-Bus

VESA Local-Bus is a peripheral bus from VESA that was primarily used in 486s and provides a high-speed datapath between the CPU and peripherals.

VMM

(Virtual Memory Manager) The Windows XP Professional system component responsible for managing physical-to-virtual memory mappings and virtual memory assignments.

VoIP

(Voice over IP) A Voice over Data implementation in which voice signals are transmitted over IP networks.

VPN

(virtual private network) A secure and private network connection that you establish either between two LANs or between a user and a LAN over the Internet.

VPN protocol

Protocols that provide VPN functionality.

WAN

(Wide area network) A network that spans multiple geographic locations, connecting multiple LANs using long-range transmission media.

WAP

(wireless access point) A device that provides connection between wireless devices and can connect to wired networks.

wardriving

A popular way to gain unauthorized access to a network that involves simply driving in a car with a laptop and a wireless NIC until the NIC detects a wireless network, which according to some reports, is very easy in large cities.

web browser

A software application used to locate and display web pages.

WEP

(Wired Equivalency Protocol) Provides 64-bit, 128-bit, and 256-bit encryption for wireless communication that uses the 802.11a and 802.11b protocols.

WiFi

The popular implementation of the 802.11b wireless standard.

Windows desktop

A general term for the overall contents of the computer screen that displays whenever Windows is running.

Windows security policies

Configuration settings within Windows operating systems that control the overall security behavior of the system.

wireless communication

Network connections that transmit signals without using physical network media.

workgroup

A Microsoft network model that groups computers together for organizational purposes.

worm

A piece of code that spreads from one computer to another on its own, not by attaching itself to another file. Like a virus, a worm can corrupt or erase files on your hard drive.

WTLS

(Wireless Transport Layer Security) The security layer of WAP, providing mutual authentication and data encryption.

WWAN

(wireless WAN) A computer network that enables users to wirelessly connect to their offices or the Internet via the cellular network. (In contrast, in order to connect using a Wi-Fi adapter, you must connect wirelessly to an access point that is wired to connect to an Internet service provider.) WWANS are sometimes referred to as wireless broadband.

XIP

(Execute In Place) A PC Card feature that enables operating system and application code stored on the PC Card to run directly from the PC Card rather than executing in RAM.

ZIF socket

(Zero Insertion Force socket) A type of processor socket that uses a lever to tighten or loosen the pin connections between the processor chip and the socket.

Zinc Air

Portable computer battery that uses a carbon membrane that absorbs oxygen.

ZV

(Zoomed Video) A connection between a PC Card and the host system that allows the card to write video data directly to the VGA controller.

ACS85820LGS3PB rev 1.0
ISBN-13 978-1-4246-0471-5
ISBN-10 1-4246-0471-0

9 781424 604715

90000

A0922090408